Self Talk

A New Self-help Guide to Manage
Emotions

*(Speaking to Your Life and the Generations to
Come)*

Connie Munguia

Published By **Tyson Maxwell**

Connie Munguia

Self Talk: A New Self-help Guide to Manage Emotions (Speaking to Your Life and the Generations to Come)

ISBN   978-1-77485-491-4

No part of this guidebook shall be reproduced in any form without permission in writing from the publisher except in the case of brief quotations embodied in critical articles or reviews.

Legal & Disclaimer

The information contained in this ebook is not designed to replace or take the place of any form of medicine or professional medical advice. The information in this ebook has been provided for educational & entertainment purposes only.

The information contained in this book has been compiled from sources deemed reliable, and it is accurate to the best of the Author's knowledge; however, the Author cannot guarantee its accuracy and validity and cannot be held liable for any errors or omissions. Changes are periodically made to this book. You must consult your doctor or get professional medical advice before using any of the suggested remedies, techniques, or information in this book.

Upon using the information contained in this book, you agree to hold harmless the

Author from and against any damages, costs, and expenses, including any legal fees potentially resulting from the application of any of the information provided by this guide. This disclaimer applies to any damages or injury caused by the use and application, whether directly or indirectly, of any advice or information presented, whether for breach of contract, tort, negligence, personal injury, criminal intent, or under any other cause of action.

You agree to accept all risks of using the information presented inside this book. You need to consult a professional medical practitioner in order to ensure you are both able and healthy enough to participate in this program.

TABLE OF CONTENTS

INTRODUCTION

What do you feel like when thoughts are racing around your mind? These are the kinds of feelings that we experience throughout our lives. your inner thoughts can be a major factor in your success or failure depending on the way you approach and manage the thoughts that are that are going through your mind. The words we speak to us is important, as you are the sole one who is with us till the end of time.

Self-affirmations, or talking to yourself is what we call self-talk. I've struggled with this, too, with the years of experience and continuous repetition. I've learned to apply this in a constructive manner which helped me make improvements in my life. We're all guilty of doing this, expressing negative thoughts to ourselves constantly and it's easy to get involved with someone who can make you feel down. You can choose to closing the relationship and moving out, but you have to make that choice for yourself, you are doing it to yourself, you are expressing your thoughts. For example, when you

1

receive compliments on your clothes you might think"Oh, I've had this dress for a long time" has been there for too long, instead of being able to accept the compliments by thanking them, all of are related to the way we perceive ourselves. The way we talk to ourselves can be significant. for instance, people will tell you that you that you're not intelligent You hear this often, but eventually you believe that it is true exactly the same way you are saying to yourself. I'm not intelligent, and you begin experiencing that way. We are the ones to change our opinions, regardless of whether others give it to us or give it to ourselves.

The book we'll explore a myriad of self-talk aspects. How to utilize it to make your life better, tips and tricks for using it to be the best version of yourself. By improving your confidence in yourself, health, relationships with money, and in every aspect of your life, you will begin living rather than being a victim.

You'll learn things that are simple as you practice it You will notice modifications, but remember that you will succeed with constant effort and perseverance. This brief read will show

you how to deal with self-talk that is
positive or negative.

Based on my experience I've come to
believe that every issue has a root, and
if you deal with the root cause of the
problem, the rest will come into play. A
lot of old emotions create negative self-
talk that should be dealt with instead of
ignoring them.

After that, sit back and relax. Clear your
mind from any clutter and read a good
book.

Chapter 1: introduction to Self-Talk

What is Self Talk? Talk?

Self-talk refers to inner conversations or conversation in our heads all the time It is evident for children who play by themselves and talk to themselves. For some people , as they get older, self-talk turns into non-verbal, whereas others still speak to themselves when they enter adulthood. I'm sure you've seen people walking and talking or reciting their thoughts, if you've been a surveillance camera operator, you'll know this better. People perform this behavior without conscious note of it. The benefit of this is harnessing the power of your self-talk for your advantage.

Self-talk is something that everyone does even if we don't admit it when caught loudly

We all speak to ourselves , whether we are conscious or not whenever we think of thoughts in our heads which never stop coming back. I speak to myself constantly whenever I'm not connected to a pen or paper I am aware that I have many things in my head. Self-talk is a positive thing because it is the externalization. When you begin to write down thoughts that are happening inside your mind and you begin to notice your thoughts are more precise, and your body will become more relaxed. It's like magic. it has helped me with writing my books.

What exactly is self-talk?

Self-talk is divided into three phases: positive self-talk positive self-talk, negative self-talk as well as neutral self-talk. Positive self-talk is the positive words we tell ourselves. When we reach the goals we set for ourselves we tend to speak to ourselves in a positive way. Negative self-talk however is the reverse, when things don't go as we had planned. If when we are angry with our own self-esteem, and we repeat negative thoughts repeatedly until we believe that they are true. When they are repeated over and over again the negative self-talk starts to affect the self-image we have of ourselves, self-confidence and self-esteem. If you don't know how to make negative events that occur to you as a way to alter your life, you'll be prone to an unworthy self-esteem. Self-talk that is neutral is neither negative or positive.

Let's Take a look at three examples of Self-talk.

Positive Self-Talk

*I love myself and value myself for the way I am

* I am active I am energetic and full of energy

* I am intelligent

Positive self-talk improves confidence and self-esteem.

Negative Self-Talk

* I am born unlucky

The other friends of mine are doing better far better than me.

* I am an unreachable person.

Neutral Self-Talk

* I need to enhance my health

* I'm going to embark on an entirely new endeavor

* I'm able to be able to find a better-paying job

The self-talk neutral is factual and is neither negative or positive. Our brains process every thoughts and can discern the facts. Have ever wondered why you draw people to your life? The answer lies in the way your brain is connected to your perceptions of the world. Self-talk plays an important role in stimulating your brain, and also your overall sense of self-esteem. For instance, think about what you felt like when you got your first pay-check, or made an offer, you're content, however when it turns out the other way around you feel depressed and begin to criticize our own self-worth.

Our lives are a that we express to ourselves. Take a look at what you did to yourself today. Was you feeling positive or depressed? Self-talking can be described as what's happening in our minds or what we would like to be experiencing in our lives. We think about our present, past and the future, forming stories inside our heads. Make

a thorough inventory of your thoughts
and examine the areas where your
thoughts wander more frequently. When
you recall some old memories from your
previous relationship, and then you
think about the sadness of your
relationship ending or the success you
had during the time, attempting to
convince yourself that you'll be able to
achieve it in now or in the coming years,
you thoughts about yourself will define
you based on the story you're telling
yourself. Life is like the movie player.
They play out as movies in our lives. We
are actors and actresses of our own
world. What you believe defines your
character. Reminiscing about painful
experiences can lead to
depression. Discover what works for you
and discover the best way to be content,
while making better choices with a
greater and more real-world
understanding of the world. The self-talk
we tell ourselves is the story we create
about ourselves that unfolds in our lives
reality TV.

Chapter 2: Is Too too much Self Talk Dangerous?

Like the saying goes, anything that is advantageous comes with disadvantages as well. Self-talk is contingent on what self-talk consists of. If it is done in a healthy manner, it will benefit you. words can make as well as break you. So take care about what you speak to yourself, or allow people to talk to your thoughts, since you process the information in your mind, whether you choose to choose to accept or deny it the decision is yours. My aunt is a talker. frequently, and it causes her to become a little agitated and she tries to sort her thoughts this way and each one of us has our own method to process information.

Everyone self-talks, some do it quietly, and for certain people they speak loudly that other people can hear. I can remember my journey between Los Angeles to New York The woman who was sitting next to me in the lounge at airport was talking to herself for a long time as she was lost completely lost in her thoughts and lost in her self-talking. When you go overboard in a way that is excessive and risk a serious injury, it could be dangerous when it begins to affect your routine. If you begin to forget the things you must do and spend a lot of time in the bathroom, holding your toothbrush, and then self-talking about how you'll be late to an appointment, it's a cause for concern. When your boss requests coffee and you become distracted by self-talking about the fact that you did not add sugar. If this behavior is a constant distraction within your daily routine, then you'll need assistance.

Self-talk that is negative can be harmful when someone grew up in a highly critical environment. The inner voice could reflect the harshness of self-talk that is a result of being influenced by early experiences such as"don't make yourself look good in this crowd, no one is interested in you, there is no way you can be sufficient, and you're the complete failure. Early environments play a significant factor in this. You have many immigrants who came from other countries but became successful in America and the reason is because the self-talk shifts and as they become more determined to succeed in their new country and by focusing on positive self-talk and determination, they succeeded in achieving their goals.

Raheem moved out of Jordan from Jordan to US and we had the course of a mastermind that struck us as a connection during our conversation. As we were discussing our personal experiences and experiences, he shared an interesting story about himself which is inspirational about how his parents sacrificed everything to help him could pursue his dream. He explained that Rich in his own words, on the day I arrived in the States I was adamant about achieving an objective and set goals in my mind , and I was determined to reach them. I am constantly repeating these phrases to myself. This country is very kind to my every aspect. In less than a year I was able to begin speaking English. My rapid adapting to my changing environment has increased my progress every time. Raheem is an entrepreneur who has made it big and happily married to three gorgeous children.

It is evident that positive self-talk coupled with determination can inspire you to reach your goals. If you allow self-talk that is negative to dominate your mind throughout the day, it can result in depression, low self-esteem and worse health issues You can witness instances of people who take their own lives according to the saying"One's enemy and the best friend is within their own.

Your Personal Best Friend and the Worst Enemy

Your self-talk could be your greatest all-time friend or most dangerous enemy. Self-talk that is negative is something you must deal with since it is a part of you and only you hold the power to alter it. The brain is tuned to negative information, so look for the triggers that cause the negative self-talk you have. One way to tackle this issue is to keep an account in your journal and every any thought that pops into your mind, write it down. I've been doing this for years and it has greatly helped me. If I am thinking negative thoughts, I write them down and attempt as hard as I can to eliminate them from my head. When I write them down, it assists me in putting physically distance between my mind and my thoughts. So far, it's been beneficial for me. Habits determine us, and it requires an enormous amount of self-control and perseverance to break out of old patterns of behavior. But I'd like to advise not to be too harsh on yourself, and let it be an incremental process. Numerous gurus advise affirmations that are positive. The affirmations you choose to use must be in line with your feelings, and how you feel inside your subconscious mind, where your beliefs that limit you reside. Many people are depressed after affirming positive self-talk but no change is occurring, and they are worse off than they were before. You may affirm that I am financially successful however, deep inside your brain will be telling you that you've never paid your bills and don't have any money in your bank account. you instantly start to stir up an unrest.

If you're not confident you are more likely to find your self-esteem-boosting statements could backfire especially for those susceptible to anxiety and depression. To break old habits, you must remain mentally stable. It is essential to clean your internal environment in order for you to enjoy the results you desire whether it's your relationship, health or even your business, they will not happen overnight.

Look at the areas in your life that require improvement. Begin taking action and work on each step at one time. Our old habits are embedded in our minds It takes an enormous amount of effort and perseverance to change it into a new patterns of behavior. Things must be changed in the inner part before you can notice a change.

Chapter 3: Do positive self-Talk and affirmations work?

The world we live in is full of negative influences that surround us. These are a result of family and friends who aren't encouraging occasionally, while others do this consciously or unconsciously to maintain control and, most of the time your mind is focused on the negative remarks made to us. Look at children who were raised in a family that was violent and the odds are they will be negatively affected by it However, children who were raised with praise from their parents will have positive effects for the child and improve their self-confidence. Positive self-talk can eliminate any negative notions that you hold about yourself, as we have discussed in the first chapter, this isn't something that can occur overnight. You must keep practicing, effort, determination and actions. It's easy to talk about things, but if you keep them in your conscious mind you won't see any effect until it is residing within the unconscious mind in order to be able to see the long-term effects.

When you begin studying a subject, it's going to be difficult but as time passes, you begin becoming comfortable with it for example, when you first begin learning to drive a vehicle, initially, it appears to be an impossible job but as you progress, everything becomes easier.

Common mistakes people make when Utilizing Positive Self-Talk and affirmations

People believe that saying positive affirmations will improve their life overnight, but the reality is in this manner. It requires determination, perseverance, and the right actions before you begin to see positive results to your daily life. It is important to know the root of the problem. Reminding yourself that I am wealthy are not the best option for those with a mindset of poverty.

If you want to make an income of six figures and don't even earn a hundred dollar, then instead of blaming the circumstances. You need to examine and talk to your own inner self.

Positive affirmation is similar to mind-body programming that helps the soul. You must have a path to your goal. You must be prepared to perform the work

needed before it becomes
effortless. Let's look at these four
stages of competency.

* Unconscious Incompetence

* Conscious Incompetence

* Conscious Competence

* Unconscious Competence

Unconscious Incompetence

In the beginning you're not aware of
what you're not aware of. That's where
we hold the old beliefs, poor habits, and
the traditional patterns. There is no way
to progress with your life without the
right plan. You have put in the effort
and perseverance to get to the next
step, that is conscious incompetence.

Conscious Incompetence

At this point, your mind is aware that
you're taking a different path. This is
where the majority people stall or don't
wish to leave their comfortable zone. To
reach the next level , which is conscious
competence you must surpass your
human instincts. In this is where many

stop and give every excuse they can
think of to delay taking the actions
required to reach the next stage , which
is called conscious competence.

Conscious Competence

Your self-confidence has grown due to
your experiences in the past. Now
you're more determined and focused
and believe that nothing can hinder you.
You can are able to feel the progression
of your path. Prior to this point you've
been through numerous ups and downs,
and your outlook has changed. I refer to
it as the stage of overcomers.

Unconscious Competence

This is where magic happens, after
you've been through the rough,
uncomfortable and anger that you felt in
the beginning three phases. The
conscious effort no longer required,
things get more enjoyable and
comfortable and you can become an
expert in playing your game.

At this point you begin reaping the
benefits of your efforts and dedication
to the task. You must take the extra
mile to experience the amazing

result. Positive self-talk is a process that requires determination and willpower. The four stages are the steps you will go through to alter the old habits of thought and beliefs.

My childhood was spent with my Uncle George He is an entrepreneur unlike my father who has a at a 9-to-5 job. I was very close with my uncle, and have him around whenever I'm during school holidays. He put his money into a business that went sour, losing a significant amount of money as a result and he didn't give up. A few employees were dismissed and I am still with him and observe him through those tense moments. He was a huge influence in my life. When things get better, they pick up, but the company continues to grow and growing. It is a memory that I do not forget, whenever something goes wrong, I remember the difficulties my uncle experienced and make it a reference point to never quit.

I recall when we were on a business trip along with the senior members of his employees. Later, we went shopping. Some of them purchased expensive shoes, and my uncle bought a lower-cost one than the ones they were purchasing. I was sure he could purchase the shoes they bought. I was interested and asked him what he was thinking? He responded that Rich listen, they're not entrepreneurs they're salaried workers. In his own words the man said that it's not the cost of shoes I wear that defines who I am. It is the fact that I'm an entrepreneur, and I have goals that I set for myself. Employers are tomorrow and they could be hired again however, as an entrepreneurs money is your driving force of your company, the expertise you possess is the mechanics , and the cash is the engine in your enterprise. It is important to keep an at your assets. Like Benjamin Franklin said, Beware of small expenses. A small leak could cause a major ship to sink. Reinvest the money you earn to your company.

If you aren't equipped with the mental ability to keep up that positive attitude, that it will not be effective for you. There's a vital aspect to consider yourself as an entrepreneur: are you prepared to do work for no pay? Since the chances are that your business could fail, which is the very first step in learning. Failure is a part of the learning process.

Most people aren't educated to deal with failures which is the reason many suffer from anxiety. the process can take time and requires lots of perseverance if you wish to achieve an increase in your level of competition There is a good chance that you will be stressed.

There's a lot of buzz on social media regarding positive self-talk. However, what does for one person may not be the best for you, every thing requires time and self-discipline Your tranquility is invaluable. Do not put too much pressure on yourself. Some people have developed the ability to handle stress, their brains are able to handle it. If you don't have the same capacity for mental endurance as them you'll burn out. Keep in mind "If it's easy, then it's a child's game."

Chapter 4: What to Do to Stop Negative Self-Talk

In this chapter we'll look at ways to overcome self-talk that is negative and improve your health, life as well as your marriage, relationship and business. If you're looking through this guide, it's obvious that you're not feeling great about yourself, and you're determined to make changes and I'm here to tell you it's possible. The books you read can help you discover what you can do to improve your life and then put it into action No one else will be able to do it for yourself, but only you.

As we get older our negative self-talk gets stronger. The thought pattern gets deeper into the subconscious mind of our children. The first step to overcome it is the realization that it a mental inner cleansing, let's take a look at the steps that can aid you in getting rid of negative self-talk.

Examine Your Thoughts

Take a journal and split it in two columns. The left column is to deal with negative self-talk, and the other column is to talk about positive thoughts.

NEGATIVE SELF TALK POSITIVE SELF TALK

Write down your negative thoughts in the space where to which it belongs. Then, counter that idea with positive self-talk. the most effective way to look at your thoughts is to write it down. Imagine that the negative thought concerns a book that you'd like to write. Then the thoughts will be you're not able to write the book because nobody cares about the content of your thoughts Write it down in the self-talk negative column examine it and then within the self-talk section positive, rephrase the negative thoughts in a positive manner and I'll begin writing my next book idea. Then, get moving to begin writing the book.

Your greatest friend and most difficult adversaries are you, be able to see things from a different perspective regardless of how little you are able to make the effort. Always think about ways you can improve your self-esteem. Make sure your journal is secure so that no one who is not authorized to access it. be able to access it.

Engage in Selfless Service

When you are actively helping others relieves the pressure you put on yourself. you experience the world on a more profound level By helping others you improve yourself. giving selflessly will bring you joy in your heart, and love the person who is your neighbor. Find a charity that is in your community, get involved helping elderly people when you have time, donate your time, something you have or money, even give blood. Give away something and observe how fulfilled and happy you feel when being able to heal others while healing yourself.

Find Professional Help

The earlier you seek professional assistance, the better, you'll avoid the psychological damage that you've done to yourself. What ever you're going through, you've seen someone else go through the same difficulties. What are your worries? Don't wait until the situation gets worse before seeking a therapist guide to guide you. Don't allow negative thoughts to hinder your happiness. A lot of marriages don't work due to the negative mindset of the couple, change your life and live a happy life. Don't let your old experiences ruin your happiness. The future is promising. Don't hide your emotional pain by using drugs. The the time will come when these medications will no longer be effective. as they're only a temporary solution and you must dig deeper to find the root of your trouble. Be kind to yourself and let your worries go. Be aware that there are many who are struggling to reach the point you are at Be kind to yourself.

Exercise & Healthy Lifestyle

Health is wealth, have you ever been sick? It's likely nothing is more important to you more than getting healthy. Making sure you take care of your body is your duty. If you exercise regularly, it will improves your self-confidence and helps release a happy chemical in your brain that improves

your mental wellbeing and boost your
energy levels and shed excess
weight. To lessen the chances of
depression and anxiety it is essential to
workout regularly. It is the temple of
your body. It is your obligation to care
for it in order to live a healthy life and
longevity. The way you take care of your
body will plays a significant role in your
mental well-being as you feel and look
more confident about yourself.

Chapter 5: Self Talk Tricks To Develop

In this chapter, we'll briefly talk about self-talk strategies to help you develop. It is easier to defeat an adversary by turning him into friends I call this diplomacy tricks. Become an ally to your own inner critics is the game in this chapter. There are a variety of ways to take make this happen.

Identifying Your Enemy's Method

Recognizing your own weaknesses is the first step to becoming wise. The self-talk you are talking to yourself or is it a critique from your inner critic? In the preceding chapter, we looked at the best way to record your thoughts in your journal. Learn to ask yourself a relevant question. Always view a challenge as an opportunity to learn. Be sure to ask yourself a definitive question whenever you are caught talking about negative things, for instance, if those "WHY" which is making you think of negative side, what is the reason I'm not able to make enough money? What is the reason my health is declining? The reasons go around in your head. Instead you should ask yourself the "WHAT" question What could I do to earn more money? What could you do for my wellbeing? Re examine your questions. Consider this as a way to begin learning by changing the question.

Learn to be with them, but don't pay too Much attention.

The critics in your life will always try to control you. Anxiety and stress can bring out the worst in us. Emotional management is crucial to your mental health. When you learn to remain cool when things aren't working out as you would like You will be able to keep your inner demons in the right place. You don't combat aggressively with aggression and you'll lose. Every person goes through something in life, so don't get too harsh on yourself. There are times when bad times don't last as long as good times. One is always going to be one. Always remember to appreciate yourself.

Have Fun and Laugh

Know that you won't be a winner all the time There is no way to be perfect. seeking perfection can cause more stress and is detrimental for mental health issues Be at peace with your own imperfections and accept them. The ability to be patient and accepting will aid you over the long term and help you to be happy with your own self. If you are angry about issues, the world will create more issues for you to deal with.

Laughing is like releasing your mind from anxiety, it can boost your daily mood and improve your immune system. I suggest you start smiling every day to improve your mood. This is how, make a point of recollecting that hilarious moment and then use it to improve your mood throughout the entire day. Once you have made it a habit, it'll happen naturally. For instance, if you make fake yawns the first time, do it again. The second time the final one will be genuine. Therefore, learn to laugh, it is amazing.

Chapter 6: What are you telling yourself?

What are you telling yourself? Does it help you or hinder you?

The chapter begins, prior to continuing reading, you should consider what I'm telling myself about my day whether it's either positive or negativ? It is true that we are constantly telling ourselves all sorts of negative thoughts, this personal conversation is usually triggered due to our feelings, for instance, when people say negative things about us or your boss has a negative opinion about your work, or you've got thoughts running through your head , or someone has given your a nice compliment. These inner conversations are thoughts that you're thinking about in your head. And when you concentrate on the negative it can be difficult to end them. People who are successful understand how important positive self-talk is. when you see athletes utilize positive self-talk in order to increase their confidence and self-esteem and understand how to be in a winning state of mind prior to playing.

If you're feeling low or down, switch your focus to something that can uplift you. Remind yourself of your previous

successes as a way to remind yourself
that you are able to succeed, and do not
let yourself down make use of any
affirmation you find appealing, or words
that lift your mood. Examine yourself
and see if there may be something that
you excel at, so stop feeding your
negative thoughts fuel to feed and afflict
you. You can't have people who are
shorter and taller than you all at
once. Concentrate on your strengths the
things which make you feel alive and
observe how it can increase your energy
levels for the rest of the day.

Repair your inner dialogue and repair
your life, acknowledge your mistakes in
the past and move forward. Improve
your performance by using positive
words. If you're unhappy with your self-
esteem, there's something not right with
you. You need to be able to be
motivated by yourself. We are all too
concerned about what others are
thinking about us, but that shouldn't be
your main concern.

When you think of the people you love
and you think about their issues you are
unhappy as there's nothing you can do
to assist them. You can always be
praying for them. but don't allow those

thoughts to burden you or get angry, but there is no way to fix the situation, just take a step forward.

The way we view our self and what we talk to ourselves constantly determines what we accomplish in our lives. Everyone has affirmative and negative self-talk beliefs about ourselves. We decide which one is our dominant mental state. What type of self-talk do would like to hear? You can then reprogram it.

Your emotions stimulate your Inner Voices

Every person is equipped with a filter that allows us to discern what we are telling ourselves about ourselves. Our mood triggers negative self-talk. If you're unhappy with your self, it can cause a number of negative inner critics , and are a common problem for people who suffer from every day. Internal critics that are negative have put to many individuals to be in a state of depression. A lot of people living in American suffer from depression. The negative emotions like fear or jealousy can be powerful when you get intimate with these feelings. It's important to

have challenging experiences in order
to build up mental strength. For
instance the two of them. A and Mr. B
both lost their jobs that same day. In the
case of Mr. A sees it as an opportunity
to begin his own businessand is able to
start researching innovative business
ideas. the Mr. B will feel depressed and
blame everyone else and blaming those
who listen and guess what, he is more
in a negative self-talk.

In this case you can see that you can
see that both Mr. A as well as Mr. B
shared similar experiences, but their
self-talk differs, it's not about what
happens to you , but rather the matters,
it's what you're saying to yourself. Find
ways to filter your thoughts and then
figure out how you can get the most out
of it.

Do more positive self-talk

It is easier to improve when we do the
same thing over and over until it
becomes a an integral part of our
mind. The key is to practicing, practice,
and practice. Make time for yourself and
begin writing down everything you would
like to accomplish you want to
accomplish, whether it's to enhance

your health, shed weight, or improve your business, or even your personal growth. Write down positive affirmations you'll continue to repeat to yourself whenever you feel that your negative self-talk is creeping in, take it off and replace it with positive thoughts. For instance, if your aim is to maintain healthy health, you can apply these affirmations.

* I am a lover of myself

* I take care to treat my body in a respectful manner

Every day I am getting stronger and more powerful.

* I am looking younger day by day

* I enjoy exercising my body

Start working to improve yourself. You can begin with exercises, jogging, or whatever will boost your confidence, but you must follow it with action and join groups. There are numerous local meetup groups that you can join. Do something that can make you feel better about your self.

Your personal growth is entirely yours to use the appropriate words to describe yourself. These words will form and shape your life. God can't give a man the power is his ability to accomplish for himself. Consider this question for yourself What negative self-talk do I have? Am me who is saying it to myself or allowing others to talk about negative things about me that cause me to believe that I am an unnatural way? If you are aware of what triggers the emotion, you need to you can find a solution to it , and then begin to build more confidence in yourself, which can result in more positive self-talk.

Chapter 7: Develop your self-talk and self-confidence by conquering your Mind

In this chapter, we'll examine ways to defeat your mind. The initial thought that pops into your head is: are you mindful or conscious? Consider it for a moment before we begin by separating them and how this can help you to conquer those thoughts that flow through our minds. Your mind is like a troll and can pull off a variety of tricks against it. We'll explore ways to control your thoughts.

Mindfulness of thoughts

Mindfulness refers to being aware of your thoughts. When you are aware of your thoughts, you are able to control your mind. It is a state of being completely present moment of what's happening by focusing your attention on a single thought can help you to control your mind. You can master the art of being focused on this thought at a time for 5 minutes. Be alert whenever other thoughts appear to be creeping in Meditation is an effective practice to assist you in staying focused.

Practicing Meditation

A ten minute meditation each day will help you feel calmer and relaxed. It also helps you feel in control of your thoughts the majority of the time and leads to a calm state of mind. In this state of stress, the it is possible to relax and the stress-producing activity of the brain is reduced by this practice. It will aid in focusing better and allow you to focus and improve your performance. Meditation can ease anxiety and depression, and helps increase concentration and memory.

Breathing Exercise

Breathing exercises will help reduce anxiety, stress improve your mood, and help you sleep better. The exercise is easy to do when you know how to do correctly and do not require any specific tool. The belly breathing process is simple and restful.

Find a position that is comfortable for you, breathe with your nostrils, allow the breath fall into your belly, take a full , deep breath and finally breathe out. Repeat this exercise for between 5 and 10 minutes, with your muscles relaxed and, if possible, closing your eyes. Let all tension and stress be released with the exhaled breath. This way, you'll feel more relaxed. This simple exercise can calm your mind. If your mind is in the right place. Your self-talk is more positive. and you will be able to focus on the present. The past is gone and there's no solution to it.

Mind Full of Thoughts

We live in an digital age; people are causing more anxiety, stress and negative competition that is impacting their lives. Social media can be utilized positively by joining groups that encourage you to do your best instead of using it to overload your mind with negative messages. If you are already depressed, you're doing more damage to yourself and creating negative self-talk by filling your head with the negative thoughts you read in social networks. Make time for things that positively impact your life.

Many people only share their best moments on social media. everyone has their struggles too. It is a mistake to compare your life with others. negative experiences can affect your mental wellbeing, particularly those who suffer from anxiety. It will impact the way you see yourself. Don't let the glamorous lifestyle that you are seeing take your attention away. Spend your time and energy on building yourself up and achieving your goals. This way , you'll be able to appreciate yourself and stay clear of self-deprecation that could cause stress due to unneeded issues.

When your thoughts wander to everything that distract you from the present moment. Invest your time and energy in yourself. This is the place you'll live throughout your life. Those things that do not help your personal growth, eliminate them. Maintain a healthy relationship, particularly with your spouse, when you're married, and also with your friends who are positive. The mind of yours is your property spiritually and it's your responsibility to guard it from negative thoughts from settling into. Get involved in something that is new to you for example, such as learning a different language, registering in a classes in music, or attend seminars and gain new knowledge that can have an impact upon your lifestyle.

Chapter 8: Self-Love's Power

How do we define Self-Love?

This chapter we'll look at how self-love impacts the way we talk about ourselves, and our relationships with other people, as the saying goes , you can't give away what you don't have. What can you do to love yourself self-love when you don't feel like you? The mind, body, and soul are reflected in our health, self-love is the basis of positive self-talk. What do you think of yourself? What are you saying to yourself? The questions you should consider: what have to say to myself, is it encouraging or depressing? Take a moment to think about it and examine these questions, you'll discover the solution to your issue. When you are able to recognize yourself, you will be able love your neighbor , who is also thyself. every person you meet is a reflection of what's happening in your own life. what you admire in someone else is the just as what you don't like about them.

Why is Self-love So Important?

Self-love is a must in our lives as it forms the core of who we truly are. how we treat and love others. However, we tend to concentrate on other matters and often overlook an important aspect in the daily lives of ours. People go through life trying to conform to be liked by others to feel more comfortable with them. The truth is, once you begin being happy and grateful for yourself, others will behave similarly so that you don't seem to be in need of approval or awe from others. If you are a person who loves yourself, and appreciate the human spirit, and treat others as you would like to be treated. You establish limits and strive to achieve your goals. self-love. Self-love creates confidence and happiness. Spending time with yourself boosts self-love. Self-love will help you be able to overcome obstacles. You will get that knowing that things will improve over time. If there is pain but joy , it is evident that the pain won't last forever.

Self-love is a problem that has led to many issues within our daily lives. relationships, health, and marriages. Many marriages have failed due to a lack of self-love that leads to self-talk that is negative. Self-love is a crucial aspect of our relationships because you view your spouse as a reflection of you. A large number of couples are in a depression. Insufficient communication, not enough good time, for the guy, his sexual desire will be diminished to the point of being non-existent. A family divided is not sustainable and divorce is at one of the main reasons which causes a lot of people to be in depression, and some are left suffering from guilt and depression, and even some who will never come back from it, do not let these things make your marriage a mess. Insufficient self-love by either spouse can result in stress and discontent on the part of the couple.

What is the importance of self-love?

Self-love is the first step to self-mastery. This results in a high self-esteem, self-confidence and self-esteem. Be aware of the fact that no one will be more devoted to you than you. Self-love sets the standards for how others will treat you. If you are able to love and appreciate yourself, you'll feel more confident and happy. The more you cherish yourself and increase these characteristics, which help you develop a positive mindset. If you don't love yourself, you'll always be a victim to life, instead of being a winner. Self-love can help you grow.

Your inner strength

The inner strength of a person is their capacity to manage the pressures we face in our lives. Without self-love, it'll be difficult to develop inner strength to conquer adversity. your inner strength comes from within you and the more you value yourself the more you inspire the people who surround you. It is impossible to build inner strength without facing difficult challenges that will bring you closer to your own your own freedom. Life's obstacles are not intended to cause harm, but to build you up.

Improve your mental well-being

Self-love can improve your psychological well-being. If you're healthy mentally, you can live your living life to the fullest. and your health as a whole is among your most important asset. Loving yourself will enable massive mental growth. Many people suffering from stress because of their the lack of self-love which is affecting one's health slowly. As I said in the previous chapter , learn how to smile, it can do amazing.

Adversity can be a step to greater accomplishment

The ill fortune can be a catalyst for self-improvement and growth. You can see the positive of every challenge that confronts you. There's nothing that you can accomplish in life without having to go through hardship. We are grateful to those who have achieved great successes in their lives however we haven't thought to consider the challenges they endured when they were in awkward situations in life. However, they believed that things will only improve with time, and without self-love, you'll soon abandon your goals.

Enhance your marriage

The union of marriage can propel you to higher levels of achievement. Self-love is the basis of an effective marriage. Whatever you wish to achieve in marriage has to start with yourself. Stop accusing and blaming your spouse. It is easy to blame your spouse rather than take responsibility for your own actions. Everything you wish for from your spouse should begin with yourself. The basis of marriage is sharing happiness. When you are happy with yourself you will be able to appreciate your partner. Self-love is the most important factor to finding the true self-love. Everything depends on self-esteem, self-control, self-confidence respect for yourself, self-esteem, and self-worth All of this is about identifying your authentic self. Once you realize this and your self-talk becomes more positive. You transmit this message to others unconsciously by the message you're communicating. You might not realize that, but you're constantly sending messages, either positiv or negativ. Signals that define you to your partner. Your attitude towards yourself is a major factor in how others communicate with you as well as treat you. Everything begins with you.

Chapter 9: Enhance your self-confidence by encouraging positive self-talk

In this section we will explore how to boost your self-confidence using positive self-talk. Many people do not realize of their constant thoughts. In reality, we all engage in it daily and it is this mind-based self-talk which gives instructions to the subconscious mind that carries these orders. Our actions are greatly influenced by the thoughts we create in our minds. Are the negative thoughts that you have about yourself affecting your life? Remember that thoughts are the basis for words and out of words is action. If the thought that goes around in your head are constantly negative, your subconscious mind will carry out the commands you are in secretly directing it to do so, regardless of whether you're aware of whether or not it's doing the work for you throughout the day.

As an example, you might find a stunning Rolls Royce with a beautiful interior. Everything is perfect however, without a functioning engine, the vehicle isn't able to function properly. The subconscious is your motor of your life. You must understand this and begin working to enhance your self-talk so you

can live your ideal life. The way we live
our lives is similar to film that plays out
each day if you know the workings
behind it, Then you begin to shape your
life. Have you ever been to an audition
for a film before? Before a film can be
released there is lots of editing that are
done to make the film enjoyable. You
don't need to look at the flaws which
were hidden behind the scenes which is
the way your subconscious mind
functions. It is your subconscious that is
the unnoticed control of your life, and
when you begin to give it the right
message through positive self-talk,
that's where the magic begins to
unfold. People say that"my friends
always" and they are blessed. I'm going
to reveal to you the truth. Your friend
know how your subconscious mind
operates and is feeding it the right food
for your mind which is your thoughts.

All it takes a consistent practice. The
majority of individual's mental chatter is
negative. However, the reality is that
you can modify the way you think. Are
you feeling guilt over the past or
anxious over the coming days? Would it
be possible to alter your internal
conversation? Then, you can alter your
actions and start generating different

results for yourself. Change the way you think about yourself and begin to affirm positive self-talk, you'll improve how you think about yourself. These suggestions will help improve your self-esteem.

Concentrate more on your individuality

The majority of people dwell on the things that they do not like about themselves and this thinking continues to recur until it is a an integral part of our mental model and focusing on the things that make you feel alive. If there's something you are better at than the rest of us, and learn to appreciate the virtues of your character. Make yourself a cheerleader and you'll see your self-confidence will begin to grow. Your inner strength is what makes you shine, so don't be concerned about what other people are saying about you, you should focus on your strengths. The trick is to discuss the things you love about yourself and you'll notice how this positive energy can influence the people around you, and how they feel about the non-verbal message you're communicating. What you like about yourself will increase your energy levels and make you'll feel more youthful and energetic every day. In the society we're leaving behind, you'll meet people who will critique your actions however, you are not doing it to yourself. Explore your innermost being to find your own uniqueness, and then build your confidence around this, and eventually it will be a part of you.

Love Yourself unconditionally

Being kind to yourself and accepting yourself can bring greater abundance into your life. When you feel good about yourself you set the tone of how other people will treat you. Being happy with yourself means being comfortable with who you are. You are aware of what you are good at and weak points, and you are at peace with yourself even when you're facing challenges in life and you are aware that it will ease. Self-love lifts your spirit and makes you in a position to inspire others positively.

Do not listen to those voices Within Your Mind

Your mind is able to play tricks on your mind. It is important to realize that your mind is an instrument. When we connect with those voices taking place in our minds when we feel that we do not like ourselves, but remember that not the real you. It's your mind. The brain is an instrument that can be used, but don't allow your mind control you. If you ever hear negative thoughts, remember that it's not you, it's the mind feeding you a negative beliefs. There is something special about you that is unique to you. Nobody else can achieve better than you. Be quiet because your mind does not know what it is talking about. Your mind is always trying to imagine a solution that's not present. If you can do this more frequently, your self-confidence will rise.

Put on a nice outfit

Are you aware that appropriate attire can increase confidence in yourself? If you dress like someone who is pursuing a particular goal within their life, this improves confidence and self-image. the actions you take have a major influence on your character. Many entrepreneurs work from home and it's essential to dress as if you're in work in an office. It isn't a matter of whether your work is from home or not., these actions establish a certain set of standards for yourself and enhance your day-to-day activities for the entire day. Don't wait until you lease an office space, and begin dressing yourself well. my suggestion is to dress as you'd like to be perceived, even if you work at home. Be sure to dress like a queen or king it's not a bad thing. Things you think don't matter, they really do matter significantly. It is a common belief that once I earn that amount of money , I'll start wearing a nice outfit, but unfortunately it's not that way. Begin today. Your subconscious mind is able to understand your feelings and emotions. Dress yourself as if you are to make yourself look like an effective boss. Dressing in the right way communicates the status of your self, confidence and wealth. The more stylish you look the more effective your messages will be. Always tidy yourself up to tidy up your home.

Chapter 10: What are the reasons to focus on the positive?

Why is it important to be positive?

There are many people say to be optimistic and concentrate on the positive aspects of life but nobody can clarify the motivation for this. You may be asking yourself why I should be optimistic. Let me share the many benefits of being positive. Positive thinking allows you to accept the world as they are , and provides you with the ability to face setbacks and mistakes. It is possible to view challenges and stressful circumstances as opportunities to try something completely new within your own life, by having an optimistic outlook.

Do we all want happiness? We all do and you can have it by embracing optimism to your daily life. When you're in positive thoughts and attitude, you'll experience the complete state of being in your mental, emotional physical, and social well-being. You'll be able handle anger, stress and other destructive emotions with ease. You'll begin using the negatives and setbacks as paths to correction in your life. You'd feel joy as well as enthusiasm and other positive emotions.

* Wouldn't it be wonderful to be around someone with a positive attitude?

* Do you not want to enjoy a positive relationship with your family?

Aren't you always looking for ways to be more successful in your the world?

The solution to all issues is to adopt positive mentality.

I'm not here to be boring you with the negative effects that negativity may bring to your life. Since you are aware that negative thoughts cause anxiety, self-esteem issues and no growth in the future. It also makes you feel isolated from others, and can affects your health, and alters your mental outlook. Let's concentrate on the wonderful opportunities that are available to your life by focusing on positivity.

Do you have the ability to be positive in the world?

Many people are unsure if they can achieve happiness in their lives because the process takes time, effort and effort to attain positivity. However, I can assure you that if you're willing to change your life then you are able to have an optimistic mindset.

* I'll ask you some questions to see how you can live an optimistic lifestyle.

* Do you know how long it took to become negative? (No)

* Are there people who are born with negative thoughts? (No)

* Do you learn positive or negative characteristics from your own experiences as well as the experiences of other people? (yes)

Be attentive to final question. Positive or negative both are acquired traits. The good thing is that you can train yourself to be positive and learn how to become negative. Anything you choose to repeat over and over is strengthened inside your head. All you have to do is start today to focus on positive thoughts and then act on them. The strategies within

the guide will lead you to a more
positive way of living.

Your anxieties, fears doubt, self-doubt
and the ability to change your life is in
you. I encourage you to increase your
desire to transform your life.

Chapter 11: Rethink your outlook

Life is an extremely fast-paced adventure and a lot of things take place every day that impact our lives, in a positive or negative way. It is important to understand that everything happens to serve a purpose and in some way or another it makes us stronger and helps make us stronger. Even if you aren't sure of the reasons behind it, at some point, you'll realize that the lesson was well-worth it. You'll be able to decide if decide to learn from the experience or remain in denial.

Many of us remain in denial and attempt to make amends for things that didn't go as planned. We worry constantly and decide not to consider the reason behind our failure. It could be an unresolved relationship to a project that was not completed or even a squandered promotion. We tend to be obsessed about the past but neglect to consider the causes. Not only do we decrease confidence in ourselves and self-esteem as well as, reduce the chances of living having a prosperous life.

The most effective solution to this issue is to alter your view of things. This won't ensure that you'll never fail in your life however it can protect your self from failures. A change in perspective can assist your life in the following manners.

1. You can control your thoughts

2. It will allow you to stay focused on the things that matter.

3. You'll never be the victim of self-blame and self-criticism and self-loathing

4. It can boost your mood and boost your confidence.

5. It will bring joy to your life.

Follow the steps in the following order at any time you are in a stressful situation.

1. Pause and think Pause for a second to reflect on the issue in front of you. Do not overthink the situation by thinking about the future. Refrain from the random flow of thoughts that start to overwhelm your mind and they can make you feel anxious.

2. Review the situation Once you've established an equanimity, attempt to think about your strategy and the possible outcomes. Be aware of your mood and your ability to manage the current situation. Be conscious of the tone of your voice and body language and the way you think as you make your decision to behave. If you don't feel confident regarding your decision do not proceed further.

3. Change your focus If you aren't sure that your decision can result in an outcome that is positive, you should try shifting your focus. It's easy and efficient. You don't need to be a shrewd person, just make sure you speak with respect smile, be kind try accepting, and get help when needed.

Think about whether this will have any impact in a year?

If you find yourself facing a stressful circumstance that makes you be worried and to think negative, consider how the situation affect your life. What will it mean in the next year? If no you should put it aside and approach the issue in a more positive manner.

Let's suppose that your friend was rude to you and was rude. What do you do now? Are you going to argue? Do you challenge her? Are you going to speak with her in a disrespectful tone? Do you worry about it? Do you feel guilty or blame yourself for the situation? You might be contemplating one or more of the options above to take revenge. However, I suggest that you be patient and think about whether this behaviour be a problem in the future? It won't impact your life in any way following one year.

Sometimes, people (most of the time) behave in ways they aren't intending to do and do things that they wouldn't want to. Don't be too eager to react to hatred, negative comments or indecent actions. Even if you do fail at something, think about whether it is too difficult to conquer? If not, then you can deal it with a positive attitude.

Chapter 12: Practice mindfulness

Before I explain how to practice mindfulness I'll introduce the notion of mindfulness. Mindfulness is a relic of meditation that was utilized through Buddhist monks. In the present, mindfulness is the most reliable method of achieving the state of complete happiness. Mindfulness is the ability to be aware of the present moment and live the present moment completely. I can assure you that mindfulness can improve your mental, emotional physical and social well-being. If you're not convinced then let me share with you about the life-changing benefits of mindfulness.

* Reduces stress, anxiety and depression

* Lowers the risk of chronic pain, blood pressure and other lifestyle-related diseases.

* Aids in treating Alzheimer's disease, and delays the onset of Alzheimer's disease.

It can assist you be efficient and innovative.

* Be more socially and emotionally stable

* It can assist you become more aware of yourself and more focused.

Are you unsure about the effectiveness of mindfulness?

I'm not judging you, it is a common misconception that people question the effectiveness of mindfulness as when we hear meditation, a feeling of boredom and ineffectiveness is triggered over us. I am confident that mindfulness is more than simply meditation. Meditation isn't the only method you can be mindful. You can pick one of the methods listed below according to your preferences and level of comfort.

* Yoga

* Walking

* Meditation

* Journaling

* Self-talk

* Gardening

* Knitting

* Any other task that you love and are able to accomplish easily.

What are the reasons to practice mindfulness?

We live in a perpetual state of stress all day long. We are worried about our present, our future, as well as about the lives of others' past and their future. Aren't we wasting a lot of our time and mental power? It is, and we're well conscious of that however, we are unable to not stop worrying. In addition social media can increase the number of people we can connect with who live lives like us, which can turn our anxiety into a state of agony, even anxiety. Mindfulness helps your brain be present in the moment and ensures that you don't live your time in a state of mind reality. If you're not filling your thoughts with images of the past or the future, you will be able to make the most of your current. Because it's just in this moment you can heal your past and improve your future.

Additionally, mindfulness can help you become more conscious of your needs for emotional support, which can makes you more secure. It's not only a pastime. It's an approach to living. It is possible to say goodbye to your fears of the past and your future by the time you begin to become conscious. It's an all-mind game and your mental state is where all your worries as well as your confidence and the capacity (belief) to transform your life. Be aware and aim to reach every day to new heights.

What can you do to practice mindfulness?

Every day, take 5 minutes to be calm and still. Be aware of your thoughts and feelings without judgement Let them flow freely. Do not question your thinking process, allow the thoughts to move and flow. Be more attentive in the present moment. It's possible to do this while you shower, walk or eat or when you meditate. It is your choice to choose the best method for you. When you begin to practice mindfulness it will be effortless to you, however you'll require time and energy to master this skill.

You can eliminate the negative images that pop up to mind by being aware. You can also change your approach to reacting towards positive from negativity once that you're aware of your feelings. When you are aware, you don't let your feelings go like hate, anger or jealousy.

Mindfulness can be utilized throughout your life. For instance, let's discuss the advantages of mindfulness in relationships. If you are mindful in your relationship, you'll be able reduce and manage conflicts. Your awareness would be of social, emotional and physical demands of your partner and your own, which will help be able to overcome jealousy, miscommunication and attention deficit. You'd be able to communicate effectively and remain aware of your actions. I hope that you comprehend what I'm trying to get at In short you'd enjoy a satisfying and satisfying relationship.

Therefore, I've provided you with the tools to help you live a better life. I'll let you to discover its advantages.

Chapter 13: Critique and setbacks shouldn't be bad for you.

Setbacks, criticism (failures) aren't always a cause for concern. What is the first thing that comes to your thoughts after hearing this sentence? If you are of the opinion that criticisms and failures are a sure way to cause nothing but loss of confidence in your life, then I encourage you to consider this issue from a different perspective. What thoughts are in your head when you think about the questions below?

Can you estimate the amount of inventions that occurred accidentally? (most aren't)

* How many famous celebrities and politicians have overcome negative criticism? (most all)

Do you remember stopping your studies when you were given a low mark at school? (no.)

* Did you make a learning from a mistake that you made? (I did)

Thus, criticisms and failures are a necessary element of your existence. Sometimes, negative

feedback can inspire you to take a
different direction, inspire you to be
better in it, or could cause you to
become better in it. When things don't
go your way do not believe you're
insignificant or that you aren't able to do
it. Maybe you have to think about it in a
different way or perhaps take a risk and
try something different. There are
numerous life-changing stories that
show people who took their negatives
and made use of them to improve
themselves.

Criticisms and setbacks are actually
teachers, and they can help you become
better at what you do. I believe that
criticism and failure always precede the
achievement. Don't view criticism as a
stop-sign in life. Instead you should
view criticism as speed bumps. What do
you do if you come across speed
bumps? Do you put your car in a stop
and wait there for a while because it
made you slow your speed? No! It's not,
you go through the traffic light and then
accelerate. This is the way you should
conduct yourself in the world If you do
fail in your life, you should take the time
to discover the reason for the failure ,
and then work through to fix the issue.

What should to do when you are boss is giving you poor feedback in the office? You want him to clarify the error, and you ask for assistance from the team, or work to become more effective at the task.

What should you do if you fail on a test? You go back to your study and pay attention to questions you weren't able to solve.

When life blesses you with a sloppy critic, Accept it, look at the situation, and then rewrite it the best way you can.

Chapter 14: Get rid of the negative breeders

It's fun to eliminate the negative people in your life, however, it's a little bit difficult to understand. You must recognize them, take action and devise methods that aid you to eliminate the influence they have on your daily life. You've been warned that you can't remove the negativity causes, but the way they control your life. Everyone has enemies and those who attempt to make us fall every turn.

Negativity can manifest throughout your life. It could be found in your family, home friends, relations, relatives work, or even inside yourself. The best part is that you will be able to be able to recognize and tackle the issue.

How do you spot negative people?

Negative people always wear an unflattering image around them. Sometimes, we can identify the negative people based on our instincts, but most times, we aren't aware that they're in control of our lives. Here are some tips you should remember when you are trying to identify negative people.

1. They broadcast gossips and negative news.

Negative people are fond of discussing their lives and spread gossips. They will show up or make calls and talk about a tragic incident, bad news they've heard, or secret information. If the conversation begins with "don't divulge to any one" or "did you have any information about" or "did you hear about" it's an obvious sign that someone wants to inform you of something that is negative. These people are known to love gossip and draw attention through sharing gossip and negative news.

2. Can't-do attitude

Negative people are able to convince them and others that everything is unattainable and impossible to achieve it. If it's a picnic, conference or an event that you're looking forward to you'll be able to find a method to make you feel miserable and convince you that it's impossible to achieve.

3. Depressing and dull.

Are you aware that certain people have a tendency to be in a bad mood? They aren't enthusiastic enough to get things done? even in mornings, or after a long vacation, they are being tired and lacking energy.

4. We can't be content for anyone.

When someone is successful in their lives, they begin to feel anxious and sad. In many cases, they begin to berate themselves about their situation and then begin to denigrate another's accomplishments.

5. They could turn a great circumstance into a disastrous

Negative people complain and complain often. They will always attempt to interpret the situation in a negative manner. If you receive an appreciation for your dress They might be able to say "did truly mean that" or some other thing that won't allow you to enjoy the praise at all. They are skeptical of everyone and cannot overcome their own self-doubt.

6. They will speak for you and try to provide you with a lot of advice.

7. They attempt to restrict your choices of making new acquaintances.

8. They won't be pleased with you.

9. They can make people feel guilty if they decide to get rid of them or spend some time to yourself.

10. They complain about everything happening around the world.

Here are some of the most commonly observed signs of people who are negative If you believe you are a victim of these characteristics, don't fret we'll assist you in removing the bad guy within you.

How do you deal with negative people?

It is important to practice, be aware and a strong skin to be able to handle people who are negative. Let's begin by learning how to handle people who are negative. Keep in mind that you are the one with the ability to decide the way you feel, how you think about choices and the way you live your life. Don't allow anyone to decide your fate.

* Maintain positive mental attitude

Negative people will try to drag you down through your cycle of becoming down and miserable But you don't have to engage in this. You should realize that it is necessary to stop talking to everyone who surround you, especially when they are relatives or colleagues. However, you can deal with the negativity of their behavior by embracing a positive outlook, and you don't need to change the way they think, just respond with positivity. If you do this, the person who is negative stops talking with you or attempts to emulate your behavior.

* Don't be their therapy

If someone is telling you about their life's abysmal do not try to fix the situation by becoming their counselor. Listen to what they are saying when they're an intimate friend, and then leave the conversation with a positive note. If you become the therapist for them, they will look for ways to dump their negative thoughts on you. Make a small conversation, listen, or remove yourself from any conversation.

* Don't offer them what they want.

People who are negative usually are looking for your approval, reactions and feedback, so the best method to remove them is to avoid reacted. Do your best to dismiss their opinions and comments regarding you, since they're attacking you with negative thoughts. You are able to be positive or show compassion in responding to them. Do not advocate for their views or accept their opinions regarding you.

73

* Note your boundary clearly

Set clear boundaries regarding dates, times and other events to ensure that you do not leave any loophole for them to enter your life. When you have the boundaries clearly, you restrict your access to those who are not in your circle. If they do interfere, you'll be able to tell them that you do not like being interrupted.

What can you do to deal with the negative side of you?

If you've realized that you're an unmotivated person and are being a negative person, you should follow these steps to transform your negative thoughts into positive energy.

1. Energy isn't destroyed, but transformed

You should be aware how negative thoughts are a type of energy that is fuelled by your thoughts and beliefs. Don't try to eliminate it since you aren't able to eliminate negativity, but you are able to change it into positive energy.

2. Stop thinking negative thoughts

If a negative thought comes into your
head, don't consider it. You can shout it
out and repeat any phrase to remove
the idea from your thoughts. You can
also consider thinking about alternatives
to the negative idea.

3. Don't be too eager to come to a
conclusion

Don't be quick to judge, react or make a
decision too quickly. Be patient with the
person you are talking to and formulate
your thoughts about them. If you are in
a stressful situation, do not be too quick
to react, instead follow the pause,
consider and take action. Be patient
when deciding every issue and attempt
to end the situation with a positive end.

4. Try to think of ways to be creative.

Creativity isn't just a characteristic of
people with negative attitudes, it can
flourish in an environment that is
positive. Make an effort to engage in
creative activities which create a sense
of satisfaction and provide you with a
feeling of achievement. When you are
able to create your own mind, it is free

from worry and negative thoughts and, consequently it helps you become more positive.

It is also possible to be around positive individuals, take a look at educational videos and listen to positive podcasts, and work to change slowly. It's not like you became an unhappiness person in one day, so be aware that it takes some time and effort to make changes.

How do you create a positive physical environment?

Positive places are an excellent way to incorporate positive energy into your life. Here are a few suggestions which have always assisted me feel more calm and optimistic. Do you like coming home to a messy house? Do you feel able to welcome positivity even when you don't like any aspect of your home?

* A clutter-free house

Make sure your home is tidy, get your bed ready every morning, and make sure everything is in the space it is allocated. You'll be amazed be able to feel good when you return home to a clean and well-organized home.

* Bright colors

Choose bright colors for your walls, or on the brightly colored accessories to brighten up your home. It is also possible to use your favourite wallpapers to decorate your home. If you're in a place that's filled with the things that you cherish and cherish, you'll be more optimistic towards your life.

* Positive thoughts

Positive messages can be displayed on the wall, or on your desk, so you're constantly encouraged to look forward. It is also possible to use positive quotes for wallpaper for your smartphone or computer. When you look at positive quotes, you'll immediately feel more optimistic.

* Plants

Plants can brighten up your home and provide the room a tranquil feel. Natural beauty is the best stress reliever and can aid to boost your mood. Therefore, you should surround yourself with succulents and plants.

* Favorite scent

You can put your preferred scent as your personal perfume to ensure that you be calm and relaxed. It is also possible to purchase certain essential oils that assist in cleaning your home like patchouli, lavender rosemary, sage, and many more.

* Things with a positive memories

Make sure to place things with a positive experience that are associated with them within your space. When you gaze at these items, positive memories will trigger a positive feeling that your body experiences. It could be a book you enjoy reading, a note from a kind friend or medal you have won, or a photograph of a momentous occasion.

Chapter 15: How effective methods to feel more positive throughout the day

I'm sure that you've begun to feel happier already and I'd like to continue the idea of boosting your confidence by teaching you on additional enjoyable techniques. These techniques are easy to change and provide great outcomes.

1. Self-talk to help self-analysis

If you aren't feeling positive within then you won't be able to reflect that to the world. It's important to be secure in your own skin and believe that you are capable of doing it, if you are confident in your self. Self-talk can be a wonderful method of calming your inner voice of negativity and anxieties. Talk with yourself about your current day, the unresolved emotions you're experiencing and attempt to discuss your decisions. Talking to yourself will help you'll be able to understand your feelings in a more effective way and you'll be able take control of them.

2. Every day, you should make time to talk to yourself

You can begin to train your mind to be positive through positive self-talk. It is important to reassure yourself by having confidence and faith that you're capable of changing. At some point, your negative outlook will change into positive thinking.

3. Self-expression via journaling

A lot of times, we carry emotions and suppress emotions within our bodies, and these feelings develop and begin to influence our thoughts. Unresolved unfair treatment can cause the accumulation of anger, while repressed feelings of joy can result in depression. Now you know the importance of being able to share our feelings. It is possible to begin journaling in order to lessen the pressure of keeping everything in. Additionally, writing down your feelings is a great method to keep track of the negative emotions you experience. It is possible to identify what serves as the trigger for your negative thoughts and then take action in a more efficient way.

4. Practice gratitude

The practice of gratitude can help us feel grateful and blessed to have the things we do are blessed with. Negative thinking leads us to be unhappy about what we don't have. Appreciation helps us appreciate how fortunate we are by focusing our attention on the things we do have. It's the perfect way to overcome the negative effects of life and to feel more positive every day.

5. Make a routine for your day

A routine that you follow every day helps to feel at ease and relaxed all day long. The routine you follow every day could be whatever you want to do daily. For many, a typical ritual includes making the perfect cup of coffee writing, journaling, working out and meditating, planting a garden or just spending time with their pets. You can pick a thing that you love doing every day and make sure you keep to it. If you complete a simple task over and over again, you feel as though you're on top of the world for your life and are content doing it.

6. Exercise and eat healthy

Being active and eating a healthy diet can make you feel good about your body and overall well-being. If you feel confident that you're in good shape, you feel great, and you feel more confident about your appearance. It is important to feel confident from within , and reflect it in the external. It is possible to find a workout regimen that you are at ease with and place more importance on eating an appropriate diet.

Chapter 16: Rewire your brain so that it can behave and think differently

Neuroplasticity is a proof that you can change the wiring of your brain at any time. It's like training your brain to memorize the habit, language or a specific action. It is possible to train your brain to recall more quickly and focus on the task in front of you.

Neuroplasticity is a wonder because it alters your reactions and thoughts based on your desires. If you hear names of the person who is your least preferred person, you'd be anxious and uneasy. It is possible to change this through neuroplasticity. You can practice the desired response and then your brain will respond in this manner effortlessly.

What can you do to feel more positive through this method?

One way to get started is to use the"yes and no method, then repeat it.

1. Begin by sitting comfortably.

2. Begin to envision a normal day and go through the day

3. Then, you think about your day, the tasks and the people you'll encounter, as you don't think of any negative thoughts.

4. If you're in the middle of an opinion that is negative that you are not happy with, you decide to stop and try to recreate the experience by displaying a positive attitude this time.

5. It is necessary to repeat the entire visualization until you are positive throughout the day.

Think of the following scenarios as you imagine your day.

1. You're late to school, work or a meeting.

2. You're being treated in an unfair ways

3. You've received a negative comment from an employee

The idea behind this exercise is that if one can accomplish it mentally then you can do it throughout the day.

Chapter 17: Become an hero in your own life

It is vital to feel confident about your self to feel confident about your life. If there's a conflict between your beliefs and actions, then it is impossible to do anything positive. To ensure that there's no conflict between the inner and the outside self, you need to be more aware of yourself.

1. Make time for yourself

In the past, you've learned about techniques like self-talk, mindfulness, and self-expression. These methods will aid you get to become more aware of yourself. These techniques can also help you in identifying any weaknesses in your life , so you can improve these. The only method to develop yourself is through self-development. stay optimistic and improve your life. The techniques below to improve yourself.

2. Enhance your appearance

If you focus on improving your appearance, you'll be able to ensure that you portray an image of positivity. Wear your best clothes to ensure that you look polished and are

comfortable with your
appearance. There's no need to fret
about how you appear since you've
dressed appropriately for the event. You
can improve your posture, your dressing
sense, and body language to improve
your self-image.

3. Do not engage in unintentional
chatter or gossip.

Talking about gossip and losing-talk is
more degrading than you imagine. It is a
waste of time and fills your mind with
negativity , so be sure to stay away
from the scandals. Be sure to stop those
who come to you with negative gossip
or information.

4. Use your time wisely and spend it
efficiently

In your spare time, aim to grow through
listening to Ted talks or listening to
positive podcasts, meditation and
studying something of value. If you are
spending the majority of your time filling
up your mind with ideas, you will begin
to think positively.

5. Be emotionally secure

Be sure to express your emotions with respect and show compassion towards yourself and others. Do not blame yourself, be critical or blame yourself for anything. Instead, work to build your emotional strength to be able to take care of yourself during difficult moments. If you exhibit confidence, strength, and faith even in the most difficult of circumstances, you make the door open for negative feelings to grow.

6. Values and beliefs that you believe in.

Record your beliefs and values so that you don't violate them. People generally feel depressed when something goes against our beliefs and values. Always concentrate in doing activities that feel good to you. Do not compromise your values or convictions for someone else, as over time, the conflict in your own emotions will create negative emotions within your. Don't take a decision today that isn't right for you as you'll regret it in the future.

If you're content with your life, there is no room for negativity to flourish. Be aware of your actions and choices every

day in order to cultivate an optimistic
mindset.

Chapter 18: The reason Hugh Jackman shed Weight

My church suggested that members participate for 40 consecutive days prayer and fasting, last year I was in the dark. Who wants to give away their favorite food? People who aren't willing to give up food for a period of time? Food is used as a crutch for emotional issues as well as for social interactions.

What is the reason God ask us to abandon food for a set period of time to hear his voice? I don't think that's right. What is the reason we need to do things that will enhance your Christian lives and character? (2 Peter 1:5-8)

I recently saw an interview with actor Hugh Jackman where he told the interviewer that to play his part in Les Miserable he lost 25 pounds and was without food or fluids for 36 hours. To play the part, he needed to appear so stunningly thin and yet so unique that anyone who saw him could have been compelled to believe he was sick. Actually, his appearance was it was so different from how his usual appearance and that people around him would have thought he was sick.

Let your hand rise if you find that crazy. However, Jean Valjean (his character) was designed to appear like a certain style, and Jackman didn't complain. He devoted himself to his craft and the character and was later honored with the Golden Globe and Oscar nomination. He believed that the sacrifices were worth it, and yes, the headaches, dizziness and grumpiness that he felt was a small cost to pay for how the actor was able to portray his character.

I began to realize that there's no need to doubt God's way of working. There are occasions when God demands total dedication and sacrifice from us , and it's to improve our lives and allow us to live a life that we enjoy.

Fasting and prayer for the things we enjoy will bring us closer to God in the most beautiful way and unique. Many of the people mentioned in the Bible have been saved because they put aside their worldly pleasures to give themselves up to God.

It worked for the inhabitants of Nineveh in the time that Jonah predicted that that they'd be destroyed because of their inhumanity (Jonah 3:7-10). It also helped Queen Esther. She did not fast and prayed for three days, asking for divine intervention from God in order to save the lives of Jews (Esther 4:15-17). In simple terms praying works!

In this book, we go deeper. We look into the character discipline that our character has to face. What percentage of us think we're not able to change. It's a part of who I am. My father was very irritable and my great grandmother. that's why that's in my DNA. The good thing is that we can alter our behavior. Christ has helped us to do this. This is a wonderful way for living a life of success and enjoying life to the fullest. It's a path I'm embarking on and am enjoying.

This is where I'll share with you the power of meditation praying, praying and bringing the word of God into the world to bring life transformative changes that will benefit you and the world around you. It is altering my life, and has transformed numerous lives and will surely transform yours. The journey is awe-inspiring and awe-inspiringly beautiful.

Without Christ we have no hope. This book is not an attempt to be accepted by God. Through our sacrifice to God by accepting Christ's atonement , we become to be righteous with God.

As a child or plants don't have to think about the way it grows and grow; we don't have to think about our spiritual development, wondering how it will take place, or if I'm not in the position to have what is required to achieve it. The child eats healthy food, and the plant is fed the healthy soil and exposed to sunlight and the air, the growth will naturally occur.

In order to develop and grow within our Christian life, Christ is the all in all. We look up to him and contemplate about his goodness. He is the source of living water and is the food of the universe.

In the gift of His Son, God has encircled the globe with an atmosphere of grace that is as real the air that flows through the globe. If you decide to breathe this life-giving atmosphere then you will develop into an adult Christian with godlike traits. It's not different from the characters from the Bible. God has provided us with all the elements we require to grow as we continually think of Jesus. In the absence of Jesus this growth is not possible.

It is our right to continue to grow each day. It is possible to grow by our prayers, meditation and communicate with God's word. Meditation, prayer, and speaking the word of God will produce an attitude of obedience to whatever the Spirit of God tells for us to follow. Believing in God will motivate us to following His commands.

These are the components which will produce the cake of character, and surely that's the goal we all have? to be more successful and to be closer to God is what we're all striving for. I know that's what I'd like to achieve. It is evident that the great biblical heroes did not define their situations based on the things they saw with their eyes. They defined their circumstances according to what the scriptures of God declared about their situation. Jesus our hero of all time was always doing this. If Jesus was the one who was the son of God recognized the importance of prayer in meditation, meditating and proclaiming God's word all day long, and 365 days a year, then why should I believe that I should only do it once a week , or at any time I feel the need to.

To be men and women who can move mountains, our attitudes need to evolve. The way we think about our lives and our surroundings must change. It doesn't require geniuses to figure out the best way to accomplish this. The Bible has the solution.

It states that God by his power has provided us with everything we require to live our the life we live on earth (2 Peter 1:3) Yes we, as believers in Christ we have been blessed with everything we require to develop godly character. When we make changes to our lives and surroundings, they will begin to alter. Christ died for us in order to give us minds that are positive of all things that are true honest, right beautiful, pure and of good character good character, virtue and worthy. (Philippians 4:8) It is important to meditate, pray, and speak the words of God to allow our minds to transform from negative thoughts to positive. Both of us must do our best to achieve this.

Prayer

Dear God. Thank you for filling me with a love that is eternal. Help me understand the importance of prayer meditation, meditating, talking and observing your words. It's not something I'm accustomed to however I ask that you will help me be open to it. I am sure that you're eager and willing to join me on this journey of getting understand you more. Help me understand that everything I am doing is to strengthen my character. This is the only thing I'll be able to take to heaven.

Thank you for taking the time to listen to me.

Write your own personal thoughts about what's in your head

Amen

Chapter 19: You're Not an Accident"

You are not just a chance that was born into the world.

No matter the circumstances surrounding my birth and mine, the Creator of our souls created us with a purpose. He made us to live living life to the fullest. Christ declares In John 10:10, that "my mission is to offer them a full and fulfilling life".

Truthfully, I've had the privilege of being a Christian for more than 30 years. Positive things have definitely happened however, I'm not able to over the past 30 years reach out to my heart and say that I have had a full and fulfilling life.

Divorced, raising kids by myself in a nation which isn't my home of birth, so having no relatives nearby I was financially overwhelmed at times being overweight and not professional having had the experience of being the "head instead of tail" I was feeling like life had thrown a few lemons on my path.

The Ah Moment The Ah Moment Dropping of the Penny

Then I got that "ah!" moment (thank that
the penny fell). I learned how to make
lemonade with the lemons I've sprinkled
around my life.

In spite of being on this the other side,
Christ was telling the truth when He
saidthat He came to us so to give us life
and enjoy it to the fullest. Christ has
provided everything we'll ever require in
our lives to avoid being in the way of
the potholes or lemons that are thrown
at us.

2. Peter 5 3-4 says:

"His supernatural power has provided
us all we require to live and be godly
through our understanding of the God
who has called us by his grace and
glory. In these, he has offered us his
amazing and valuable promises, so that
you can take part in the divine nature
and avoid the evil in the world caused
by bad desires."

The secret that is well-known by many
others who live their life to the fullest
and continue to live it but was elusive to
me throughout my Christian life was
believing and trusting that God gave me

all the things I required to lead an abundant life.

The Bible says that God has made us through His word, great promises for living an abundance of life. We were created and saved to be part of his divine nature. We and you have been granted the right to possess a personality as his. This way we can enjoy the life.

I don't have to be an unhappily scrooge. I could have a chance to be hopeful for the various challenges in my life: fat however losing some weight complaining but finding the courage to praise unworthy, insecure but learning the how to be grateful and negative speech, trying to say positive things of life, conflicting but making progress in becoming an peacemaker, inconsistent but gaining the ability to be consistent and financially challenged, but developing financial discipline and trusting God with the promises of Deuteronomy chapter 28. I will loan to many, but I will not require borrowing.

Join me in this thrilling transformational journey that so many have experienced. Change begins with faith and trusting in the God's word. God.

Chapter 20: The One Thing that changed My Daughter

I've put my trust in your words (Psalm 119:114)

I was wondering what was the reason my daughter would lie and acting stupid, foolish and ignorant. The answer, unfortunately, was between my chin and my nose… using my tongue.

Incredibly often, when she committed something wrong (and often it was lies we had to deal to) I would say that she was a fool, a liar and yes, the father of all lies was the devil.

I, who was a Christian I was just repeating the way I had been raised. I never thought about whether this was not true. Of course, I loved my daughter dearly. I would be willing to die for her, however I was always frustrated by the character the character she played.

My Tongue The Problem, My Tongue

In my tongue, I was killing her and gradually but surely changing her perspective of the person God declared her to be. He saw her as beautiful and beautifully made, whereas I argued with her about the opposite.

I fasted, prayed, screaming to the moon and tried all kinds of drastic measures you shouldn't be aware of however my daughter did not change.

Our weaknesses become God's chance. At my end, things began to shift and I began to pray in a different way.

I learned the power of God's word in the living word of God. It is the power that energizes my faith when I pray, affirm faith in God's Word.

My daughter began being very different when I began to incorporate God's word in her life.

So for instance, her propensity to lie began to change when I would reassure her in Scripture and speak words such as, "You are beautifully and beautifully created." (Psalm 13:14) "You belong to God and God has great plans for you and plans to provide you with hope and a new future." (Jeremiah 29:11) You are an honor, a blessing and a heritage God has granted me. (Psalm 27:3) I began an entirely new routine of blessing and affirming my children prior to when they left for school and then at the end of the evening. I did this by using scriptures to help me.

There are many other issues that required to be addressed and changed My greatest breakthrough was when I began faith and applying the word of God into her life regardless of what the physical environment had told me.

For a long time, I was having issues with a variety of characteristics that could be troubling to any Christian mother.

It was only when I made the massive step of prayer, speaking and affirming God's word in her life that I began to notice shifts in her behavior, and in the end, her whole life.

The Game that will get You Thinking

Incredulous and overwhelmed by the positive changes that have taken place in my life I am now becoming more aware of what I speak. What would happen if you believed God's word, and speaking his word, and concluding with His words about my character? What drastic changes would be made within your own life?

The tongue is the source to make a difference between both death and life (Proverbs 18:21) Take a look at this short exercise to see how powerful words can be. You can play this game called "Guess what I've spoken'.

The concept is that your acquaintance can tell whether the words you used were "I am worthy and strong" as opposed to "I am weak and not worthy" by the ease with which they are able to pull you down with your fingers.

Request a friend to get out of the room . make sure that they can't hear your voice. Lock both hands and then make an elongated fist. Spread your hands out and repeat 10 times "I are weak and not worthy" or "I am strong and worthy".

Invite your friend back into the room, and ask them to put your stretched hands to the floor.

Do everything you can to stop the urge to keep your hands pulled down. After that, tell your friend to leave the room . Then form a fist and extend out your hands like you did earlier. This time, however, you will say the opposite to the previous 10 times.

Don't speak after you've spoken the word you've said 10 times. What happens is that after you have said"I am weak and unworthy, "I have no strength and am insignificant" and the person who pushes the hands of your hand will discover it simpler to push your hands lower as opposed to when you used the words "I am strong and unworthy".

Your body's response is affected by the words you've spoken regardless of whether you like it or not, your body responds to the words you have spoken.

It is true that power lies in words, and it's no wonder we'll be judged on every word we say (Matthew 12:36)

The most effective thing we could imagine is God's word. God's words God has written in the Bible are powerful and transformative for the lives of those who read it.

His word regarding any circumstance is truthful since He is the only Truth, the way, and eternal life. (John 14:6) We are told that at God's beginning, there was a word, and the word was in God as well as the Word. John 1:1 The word of God is very powerful, because it's who He is.

When God says something in the bible, we are required to believe, trust and trust in the word of God. Refusing to believe his word is as bad as believing in him, because God is the Word.

God has revealed to us there are some actions we can take to make sure that we don't fail and that we receive an abundance of hospitality within the kingdom of God.

Prayer:

Father God, I thank you because you have eyes at those who are afraid of your name and whose hope is in your unconditional love. (Psalm33:18) My hope rests in you. Only you are the person who can alter me and my situation.

I am sorry for the times that I've believed I could accomplish it myself, but I have doubted with you that it is all possible. (Matthew 19:26)

I would like to have this year will be a transformational year. A time where I be able to meditate, pray and share your word about my character and my circumstances.

I am certain that this year is going to be one of spiritual development. I won't remain the same. When I reflect and look on the loving love that is my Savior Jesus Christ, I will change , and my life will be different.

I am thankful to you that through your grace and the grace from Jesus Christ, my Savior Jesus Christ you have given me unending encouragement and good faith (2 Thessalonians 2:16)

Include your own thoughts of what's going through your mind.

Quote:

Hope is able to see the invisible senses the unreal and achieves the unimaginable.

Anonymous

Affirmation:

I will place my burden upon the LORD,
and He will keep me, and He will never
allow me to be affected. (Psalm 55:2)

Chapter 21: The Divine Ingredients to Character Cake

The entire story starts Peter 1 3-10.
Peter 1 3-10 The text says:

His divine power has provided us all we
require to live a life of godliness through
our understanding of the God who
called us through his grace and glory. 4

In these, he has offered us his amazing
and valuable promises, so that you
could take part in the divine nature and
have been able to escape the corruption
of this world brought on by the evil
desires.

5 In this regard Make every effort to
build your faith the goodness of God
and goodness; and to goodness,
wisdom 6 and to self-control and
knowledge and self-control
perseverance, and to perseverance to

godliness; and godliness, mutual
affection; and to reciprocal affection
love.

If you are blessed with these traits in a
greater amount they will protect you
from becoming impotent and useless
when it comes to your understanding of
the Savior Jesus Christ. 9 However,
anyone who does not possess these
qualities is nearsighted and blind,
ignoring that they have been cleansed
of their previous mistakes.

10 So my dear brothers and sisters,[atry
to verify your call and selection. If you
follow these steps you will not stumble
11 and will be welcomed with a warm
welcome into God's eternal Kingdom of
Lord Jesus Christ. Savior Jesus Christ.

Here's a short overview of what you are
required to do, not just accept but be
sure of, regardless of the circumstances
currently in your life.

His power of God has given us
everything we need to live a godly the
life of a godly person and godliness

He has provided us with a powerful and
valuable promise which will allow us to

develop Christ-like characteristics (2
Peter 1:4)

In faith and trusting the promises to be
real We are expected to strive to
incorporate the virtues listed in our
Christian life. (2nd Peter 1:5)

Our journey will begin by believing and
relying on the words of God. This will
lead us to an intriguing life-changing
journey that does not focus on the
everyday aspects of who we're doing
instead, rather the supernatural words
of God and the things we are to be. The
way we live our lives is never the same
when we are taught to:

1. The Bible is God's word to alter our
character,

2. Ask God's Word,

3. We can affirm ourselves by God's
word.

Join me on a spiritual journey that we
will never become the same. The eight
life-changing characteristics which the
Holy Spirit promises to constantly
transform us into will transform our

surroundings too. When we grow, the things around us will also be altered.

You will be amazed at the things God is doing in your life by faith and trusting on his promises You will be transformed into a faith-filled Christian who is able to make any mountain to move!

This book will show you how you can be a pleasure doing this every day while you develop the qualities of:

1. Faith,

2. Goodness,

3. Knowledge,

4. Self-Control

5. Perseverance,

6. Godliness

7. Mutual Affection.

8. Love

Make and adhere to your daily schedule of how you'll get to get to know God better by His Word, which is the bible. Make a commitment to follow His word you are reading, incorporate His words into your life Reaffirm his promises, be faithful to Him, repent, and confess any time you commit a sin then get up and begin your journey all over with a new set of eyes.

Each devotional is a source of prayers, scriptures and affirmations (speaking the word of God to your daily life) with respect to the qualities that Peter recommends we develop. The power of positive speech and expressing the truth about your life cannot be stressed enough.

Prayer:

I am thankful to the Father for how you have provided me with everything I need to know about what I will do with my life on earth, and how I can develop an Christ similar character. I am thankful for your word since it is the source of my the life I need. There's nothing to worry me that you don't have an interest in. I am grateful for that. It's a joy to know that my smallest concern I can talk to you about it and discuss it.

I am confident that I can count on you. I am confident that you will serve me the way what you have done for apostles of the past. I will be an outstanding person of faith. I am sure you're not just willing to make this happen and you're also George Orwell. You have the power to accomplish it. My life and my circumstances will be transformed. I am excited for this journey, as you transform me into a wonderful persona which you have already a glimpse of. I am sure that once all is completed you'll be satisfied by the results!

Thank you for being honest. You began this wonderful work in me. I trust you to keep working until it's
finished. (Philippians 1:6)

Quote:

Character is the act of doing the right thing even when no one's paying attention. There are many who believe that all that's right is to pass while the one thing wrong is getting caught. -- J.C. Watts

Affirmation:

I have the potential to and will strive each day to become Christ like. I will bring the word of God in all of my circumstances today.

Chapter 22: To this reason, you should make every effort

(2nd Peter 1:5)

I was adamant about going to university with the same mindset I had in my secondary school days. My mother was an educator, I had no choice but to get fairly good grades which enabled me to get a spot in the university.

While at university, I continued my sloppy routine of not giving my best. If I was interested in something, I earned an excellent grade because I was enthused about doing my best in the subject.

However, any topic in which I didn't like the teacher or had having a lecture in the early hours of morning I didn't attend, and was not concerned about what the consequence of my behavior was. In all honesty, I'd not failed a single class, and surely, I was smart enough to get through.

My slack-minded attitude toward my classes came to an abrupt stop when I failed one of my classes. My failings led to a dramatic change in the way I conduct myself.

A surgeon cannot perform surgery
without a lot of hours of studying as an
undergraduate and sacrifice. Lawyers
and solicitors do not receive their
certificate of practising throughout the
year without proof that they've
continued to update themselves in their
field of research. It is impossible that an
Olympian can win the gold medal
without being denied of instant
gratification, work and dedication.

The same applies to the Christian
life. You can't be a true Christian
without exerting yourself or working
hard to build to make our lives more
Christ-like.

Paul insists that we should do our
best. It is essential to be
persistent. While good work doesn't
make us better, they show our character
and who we are serving.

The fruits of the Spirit is joy, love
peace, forbearance generosity, goodwill
in all things, gentleness, faithfulness
and self-control. (Galatians 5:22) While
the acts of the flesh include the sexually
immoral, impure sexual immorality,
idolatry, witchcraft and strife. insanity,
rage and rivalries, dissensions,

alcoholism, jealousy orgies and such things. We warn, just as I did before that those who commit such things are not going to be part of the Kingdom of God. (Galatians 5:19-21)

What kinds of characteristics do you see in the fruits lists? How many you find in your flesh list? Which one is superior to the others?

Both of us may be lacking but the good thing is that God's intention is to see you produce the fruit from the Spirit. Not only does He desire you to be able to produce these fruits, but He also is able to empower us and myself to bear the fruit from the Spirit. Jesus within us makes this happen.

He has done the same thing in the name of Moses, Daniel, Joshua He did this for Moses, Daniel, Joshua Paul and can accomplish the same for you too. Cowards, murderers, prostitutes and slaves are all transformed into the image of Christ.

There was nothing special about these individuals, except for the amazing God of the universe was the only God who could transform their hearts from stone into hearts that were flesh.

God is eager to make your life into a best-selling book that He is ready to write. When you put in every effort to strengthen your faith, God will multiply your efforts.

Your path is a continuous process of continuously improving these qualities. It is important to be working at it. You must set aside time to study His word every day. You must reflect on your daily actions and identify what you've done wrong, so that you can confess and affirm your daily actions with the promises of God's word. God.

Chapter 23: One Thing that Displeases God

It is also impossible to satisfy God in a vacuum of faith. Anyone who wishes to be brought to God must be convinced in the fact that God exists and is a rewarder for those who truly look for God. (Hebrews 11:6)

I took a second look at the clear blue sky as the plane glided effortlessly through the clouds. I was not just nervous but anxious too.

I was scared of flying. I had to get myself hyped before boarding the plane. Then, the turbulence began. In reality, it was not too bad, however I was imagining the most awful.

I checked out the plane again and saw that the fuel had leaked out of the plane. With a nervous sigh, I informed the lady sitting beside me.

In the absence of checking my words, she swiftly called the steward in order to take a look. To make a long tale short, she was quite angry at me since there was no fire in the air, only my imagination was in full swing. This was some time ago and I'm not worry about flying any more.

I was always uncomfortable flying because I was unsure of what the appearance of the pilot was and what condition that he was in. If he was drunk, do airlines test pilots for alcohol before they take off or just believe that they are safe? be drinking beyond the limit of legality. Is the person suicidal?

So these are the issues that I'm sure the majority of travellers don't think of, or when you do think of them, that does not stop them from traveling. They are able to have a certain belief that they will reach the destination they're going to.

Faith is a blessing given our by God to use. We choose to have children with confidence that they won't cause us grief or pain. We trust that all will work out fine.

If you've been treated for surgery, you've believed on the expertise of the medical staff and surgeon. We sleep each night, believing that we'll wake up.

A child is delighted, laughs and is happy when the father throws him in the air since the father trusts him to take him down.

God as a loving father would like us to believe in the words He has revealed to us via his words. He would like us to believe Him by His word even though

we don't find any proof of the promises
He has made.

He wants us to assert that he is the one
who has stated, and not letting what our
eyes of our bodies tell us the truth of
our situation.

During the lent season spend some time
reading the Bible and reflect on the
numerous promises contained in the
bible for you.

Here are some promises to help me stay
focused even when my body says one
thing, but my spiritual eyes must be
able to tell me something else through
faith.

His plans for the future of your life a
good thing: As I am aware of that I've
got plans in mind for you." God
declares, "plans to prosper you and not
cause harm to you. They are plans that
will provide the hope of a bright future (
Jeremiah 29:11)

If you are being hurt by someone be
strong and brave. Don't be afraid or
fearful of them, for it is the LORD your
God is the one who will keep walking

beside you. He won't let go of your side
or forsake you. "(Deuteronomy 31: 6)

If you feel that you are unable to
overpower temptation or sin My grace is
enough to you: because my power is
perfected in weakness. (2 Corinthians
12:9)

Prayer

Abba Father, I praise Your name for
being my strength. I thank you for the
fact that you are strengthening my faith.
Where I've been weak when it comes to
faith and trusting in God I am being
reformed by you. (2 12:9.)

Lord, I am putting my trust in God
completely. I will not be reliant on my
own wisdom regarding the things that
worry me at the moment in my personal
life (mention them one at a time before
Him) Proverbs 3:5

Write your own personal thoughts about
what's in your head

Amen

Quote:

The method to judge through Faith is to close the eyes to Reason (unknown)

Affirmation That my faith does not be based on the wisdom of men rather, it will be based on God's power (1Corinthians 2:5)

Chapter 24: Faith: I don't Think I'm Changeable

"For this reason alone try to increase the faith you have" (2 1:5 in Peter 1:5)

My knees were like jelly, and my mouth suddenly was extremely dry. "What is the significance of water pipes are broken" My daughter asked me in a loud voice. "As I've told mom, for the tenth time the tenant called me and told me that water was leaking from the floor of the kitchen".

The fear shook me. Images of an repair bill of PS30,000 flashed in my head I remembered my friend's story five years ago. Her story was happy conclusion as her insurance paid for her repair. However, in my instance, anxiety turned to complete fear when I realised that I had not taken care of my contents and building insurance.

To Lie OrNot To Lie?

Do I swiftly sort out my insurance, and then file an application (fraud!) I pondered this while my thoughts whirled. The temptation was very appealing. A friend came in to the library, and I was conducting some research while I was thinking about what I should do.

I shared my struggles with her, and together we asked God to intervene. While we prayed, the Holy Spirit moved me to begin praising God for the numerous promises in His word. I confessed my error of not being vigilant with my insurance and thanked God for listening to my plea. After I prayed, I felt a profound peace and peace.

I was in a position to think clearly. I could feel God clearly telling me to contact a reputable plumber and get the work done. I checked the issue myself, and after which I drove back to make plans with my plumber.

There would be no unprofessional business dealing with fraudulent claims. Sure, I needed to get my insurance in order but this issue was not something I could claim for.

My task now was to call an experienced Plummer. I had reason to doubt the credibility of the plumber I had used in the past for other jobs.

I prayed to God to show me what I should do. Since the job was urgent, I felt I was forced to contact my plumber.

God was not going to allow me to be fooled. The plumber I called numerous times and every time, the line would be cut off. He tried calling back a few times, but every time the call would go out. The call was cut for about an one hour.

While I was at my computer thinking about what to do next an enormous white van drove by and parked directly in front of my home. The front of the van was a large advertisement that read "Plumber." The next thing I knew, I was convinced strongly that I must contact the number.

I dialled the number, and within two hours the leaky pipe was fixed with a minimal cost. Then I got a window was fixed for free.

The Fear of the Unknown Induces Us to Act in a state of utter disbelief

Fear of the unknown may make us be skeptical of God and make us to do things that be shocking to us. The fear of not having a mother wife led Sara to cause unimaginable pain to her family and the their descendants.

Her idea that Abraham being sleeping in her maid Haggai did not just cause her to be miserable, but also to Haggai, Abraham and Isaac.

The conflict also caused animosity between Isaac's seed and Ishmael's which has remained to this day. Rebecca's fear of losing her favorite son Jacob was not going to be born, a boy that God promised would be the older son, would not be born (Genesis 25:19-26) resulted in her acting in deceit to make sure that the right child received the blessings.

What resulted as a consequence of her faithlessness to God was deceit and enmity between the brothers, as well as separation from her son she loved who she never saw ever again.

She was unable to believe that God could be in complete control over the prophecy God had crafted, as well as that his prophecy would have been fulfilled with no involvement in the matter.

What is it that cause you to be afraid and do things that are in opposition to the words of God? Write them down and request God to be gracious to you for the lack of faith that God is in a position to deal with this or those situations you're afraid. It's a lack of faith to doubt that God will handle your circumstances.

It doesn't please God to let us take the situation to ourselves thinking that God doesn't love us enough and that we must figure out the issue by ourselves.

God would like us to believe it in our heart that He will be rewarded for our decision to believe in him.

We are commanded to believe that God loves us and that, because of this He will bless us in ways that are beyond what we can even think about. To deny this truth is not pleasing to Him (Ephesians 3:20)

Prayer

I praise God God for you are the creator and perfecter of my faith (Hebrews 12:2) I am confident that you will help me in faith in you that pleases you. Lord

please forgive me for the instances
(mention the occasions) I've not kept
your word about my circumstances.

Lord, I'm praying that you grant me faith
in order that I do not be a doubter about
you. God, aid me believe in the
impossible things you are able to
accomplish within my own life. (Matthew
21:21) Allow me to have faith that you
are a faithful God and that you are a
great Father. I will never leave you and
you will never leave me.

Write your own personal thoughts about
what's going through your mind.

Amen

Quote:

Faith is making the first step even when
you can't know the whole path. Martin
Luther King, Jr

Affirmation

The Lord is my source of light and my
salvation Whom should I fear? My Lord
is the rock of my life. who do I have to
be wary? If an army is encamping
against me, I will not be afraid; even if

the enemy rises against me however, I'll remain sure. (Psalm 27: 1, 3)

Chapter 25: Goodness: I have bad thoughts, and I do terrible things

To this end, try to do everything you can to strengthen your faith's goodness (2nd Peter 1,)

My daughter was guilty of the same thing again. She was certainly not making progress. She would repeat the same mistakes repeatedly. I was angry and frustrated.

She ought to be more aware, I thought. What ensued was a frustrated spirit , and a long list of her mistakes like she didn't even know the consequences. The speech of condemnation went on for in silence for a good time.

God is a remarkably good God. His followers are all his. He's said "surly goodness and mercy will remain with you for the rest that you live" (Psalm 23:6).

Wherever you are and whatever your circumstances God's mercy will be pursuing you. You can't escape God's love and nothing can ever be able to separate you from the unconditional love of God. (Romans 8:38-39)

Psalm 103 outlines some of the many ways the way that God shows his goodness, love, and compassion for me and you.

1. He provides us with all the wonderful things we can enjoy in this life (vs2)

2. He forgives us all of our transgressions (vs3)

3. He cures all of our ailments (vs3)

4. Your crown is adorned with compassion and love

5. Kind and compassionate,

6. Abounding in love.

7. Never always accuses and he does not keep his anger for ever;

8. He does not treat us as our sins deserve

9. He doesn't pay us for our sins.

10. As in the sky as they can be above earth and so is his devotion to those who revere him.

As we contemplate God's goodness to us He invites us to be good to live a life of goodness. The more we ponder on God's words, pray, and ask to receive to receive the Holy Spirit to be present in our lives and our lives, the more He changes us.

We also have crucial roles to play in the characters that are changing. In today's stories to put in every effort and to put in a constant effortto add good for our own character.

The kind of goodness we see here is that we have an exceptional character worthy of praise as well as of moral excellence.

What are your ways of treating others? Do you treat others in the same way? generosity as God is to you?

The more you understand how gracious, merciful and loving God is to you The more you feel encouraged to show kindness to others.

The first thing we want to do is call those in our immediate family. Are you caring, compassionate and forgiving of yourself? The challenge for us is to try our best to be kind towards our kids, siblings, spouses and even our own friends.

You can ask God to reveal ways you can always be good to the people who are closest to your heart.

We must seek God to reveal to us the traits that He finds offensive. It was for me the complaining spirit, for you, it may be something else.

No matter what it is, whether it's pornography, a flirtatious characters, gossip, or insanity, God wants us to work hard to get rid of these people and to be morally upright. behavior.

Take a look at the character flaws you're suffering from and work up a plan to eliminate the flaw in your character. I was forced to limit the time that I was correcting my child. I had to resolve to encourage rather than criticize her when she made a mistake.

God is our Father. He's a loving God who has promised us that His mercy and goodness will be with us throughout the time In return, He wants us to not just be good to our fellow humans but to be of a good moral character as well.

Prayer

Father, I thank you for being kind to me. Lord, I thank you for being so kind to me that you chose to give your only son in the hope that if I trust in him, I would not die, but live a long and eternal living (John 3:16) I am grateful to that you have called me to the marvelous light of your presence.

I beg forgiveness for being unfaithful at these things in my own life (mention the areas you've not done well in). Thank you for allowing me to be forgiven of these wrongs , because you've said that if my sins are as red as they will be as white like snow. (Isaiah 1:18)

I would like to do well at these fields (mention specific areas). Please give me daily tips to help me make every effort to improve in these areas.

The most important thing is that I realize that, without you, I could be nothing. I ask for the Holy Spirit of God to help me to be successful in all the areas you have me to excel in.

I am grateful to you and honor your name since I am sure I will be able to improve in these areas.

Write your own personal thoughts about what's going through your head

Amen

Quote:

"Let us try to live so that when we die, that even our undertakers will feel sorry." -- Mark Twain

Affirmation:

I am able to accomplish all things (mention the areas that you are being impressed by the quality you are in) because of Him who is my strength (Philippians 4:13)

Chapter 26: Knowledge: I don't know what to do

"to know the virtues" (2 Peter 1:5)

What would you would you ask God to grant you if could be sure that He will without a shadow of doubt grant your heart's desires?

Young King Solomon had a golden opportunity to take over his father's King David's reign (I King 3:15). He wasn't King David's oldest son but God chose Solomon to be the one who would succeed his father.

There are many things Solomon could have asked in exchange, yet there was one thing Solomon learned by his mentor, David. He understood that to know and serve God deeply was all he needed to live his life to the fullest.

To be able to discern God's plan in all situations (have the wisdom of God) will be lifesaving for the kingdom of God and him. Solomon sought wisdom in prayer to be able to distinguish between evil and good.

Although he was a mature man, he recognized that, in the absence of God

the man was like the child who was
unable to leave or get into (v7)

Solomon's request was greatly
gratifying to God. God granted his
request and then said "See that I have
blessed you a wise and discerning
heart, and I will ensure that there's not
been anyone like you, and no one
similar to you emerge following the way
you." (vs12)

To put the an extra icing to the cake
God declared "I have granted you what
you've not asked for in terms of riches
and honor and honour, so that there will
never be a person as you in the royal
family throughout your lifetime."
(vs. 13.)

Here's the most kept and secret "the
reverence of the Lord is the first step to
the wisdom of God" (Proverbs 9:10) You
can only experience the fear of and
knowledge of God by studying his words
and understanding the word of God
thoroughly. Plan, plan and purpose what
you'll do to invest more time into God's
word to continue to grow in your
understanding of Him.

Suggestions:

* Plan out the length of time and dates you'll be reading through the Bible and other Christian books.

• Find a peaceful spot where you can relax and read without being distracted (I have one of my friends who is locked in her toilet)

* On the way to work, why not listening to a Bible audio

* Read the bible each when you do something specific e.g. ironing

* Plan to have a daily service with your family

Prayer

My Father, I thank you for it's not me who is the one who decided to search for you, but instead, you are always eager to reveal yourself to me and reveal your self to me.

I praise your name, because your word is eternal and strong, and more sharp than any sword with two edges that can penetrate even to the division between my soul and spirit and also of my joints as well as my bones, and is a discerning

139

of my thoughts and the intentions from my soul (Hebrews 4:12)

Lord, examine my heart and determine whether there is anything offense in me and guide me on the direction of everlasting. (psalm129:34)

Find the areas of my life that hinder me from getting to know you better than I do today. Show me the ways I could apply your this knowledge to my own life today.

I'm hungry to get to know you better than I do. Like the deer pants for the water brooks, as my soul pant in your direction. (Psalm 42:1)

I am grateful for your word that is found in the bible. I am grateful for the opportunity I am able to have and not overlook it.

Include your own thoughts of what's in your head

Amen

Quote:

Wisdom is the proper way to use knowledge. Knowing is not the same as to be smart. A lot of people know a good amount and are the worse foolish for that. There's no one as good as a smart fool. However, to be able to apply knowledge is to be wise. ~ Charles Spurgeon

The Affirmation is: Wisdom will enter to my heart as will knowledge. It will also be a delight to my soul. Discipline will guard me I will be protected by understanding (Proverbs 2:10-12)

Chapter 27: Self-Control: I'm Unable to Control Myself

and self-control, knowledge (I Peter 2:7) You have not been afflicted by a temptation which isn't common to men. God is faithfuland will not allow you to be overcome by temptation however, if you are tempted He will also offer a escape route, so in order for you to be able to stand up to this temptation (1 Corinthians 10:13)

Today I am fasting. I've tried fasting for a few days, but I have failed every time. I've consumed biscuits to the end. I gained back one pound that I'd lost.

I've decided to take up the word of God to help me to overcome my uncontrollable self-control sin. Self-control is among the fruits of the Spirit.

When our habits of physical health aren't good the mental and moral abilities are not strong enough; because there is a great sense of sympathy between physicality and moral.

You Can Control Your Impulses

Self-control, as defined by the dictionary, is the act of denial your own impulses; controlling them'

Humanity was deprived of its magnificent home due to a single unforgiveness and lack of self-control. God had provided Adam as well as Eve the best they could ever desire. Eve however was not content. To satisfy her whims, she and her husband went through a loss and, as a result, started the misery of all mankind.

Untold suffering has occurred because of humanity's inability to an effective control of the needs of our eyes and the taste. The ability of hunger has brought down governments and homes, the most renowned men and women are shamed due to this lack of control.

Kingdoms like Sodom as well as Gomorrah have been destroyed along with other reasons, because of the sin of eating too much (Ezekiel 16:49-50). Health institutions in the public sector are concerned about the rate at which we are overweight Everything and everything that the eye can see and taste is considered good.

As children of God, we must not consider with disdain the condition that our bodies are in. The standards of virtue are believed to be elevated or diminished by lifestyles of the body. Bad habits in eating and drinking can lead to mistakes in thinking and actions.

God will not allow us to hurt our health. He would like us to be in good health and that everything is smoothly with us. (3 John 1:2)

Christ began his work of reclaiming us all, right in the exact moment our parents' first encounters ended in destruction, right on the edge of hunger. The amazing life changing news for me and you lies in the fact it is that Satan lost in the plot to overpower Christ in the battle of hunger.

Christ was not willing to change the stones into bread loaves and then said "Man is not able to live solely just on bread alone but rather on every word spoken from God's mouth. God" (Matthew 4:14).

He Survived So that You and I Could Surmonte

He fought the power of hunger on your behalf which made it possible for you to conquer the temptation to eat, and control your appetite in every aspect that you are in.

Notice the beautiful words Christ used to say We and you must live by every word that originates from the mouth of God. We can both have control of ourselves by living according to the Word of God about control.

Here are some words to consider in connection with the current reading from the Bible.

The most important words to consider

1. Overtake

2. Common

3. Faithful

4. Ability

5. Escape route

6. Endure

Here is my plan of action to conquer. Keep in mind 2 Peter 1:5-8 tells us to put in every effort. What actions have you planned to to help you overcome the fear of control of yourself?

1. Drink water each hour

2. Google Scripture on self-control, and pray at least once an hour.

3. I will not glance at the counter for food in the canteen.

4. I'm not going to the grocery store today, but I will take my daughter to school.

5. After I arrive home, I will then go to my closet and ask God to bless me.

1. I'll pray for two friends that I have known have issues with controlling their self (one with food, one with pornography)

2. I'm going to have my daughter keep me accountable.

Prayer

I praise you Lord for your kindness and compassionate slow to anger and generous (Psalm 85:8). You haven't dealt with me in the punishment my iniquity and lack of self-control merits. (Psalm 103:10)

Your heart will be touched by the pain I feel when I've lost control in the areas that are laid out in front of you.

I am aware that nothing about the peace of my soul is little for You to be aware of. There isn't a single part of my dark story that is too dark for You to read, and there is no mystery that is too hard to solve.

You Lord are aware of my anxious thought processes (psalm 139:23) regarding this particular part of my life I require self-control in. (Be specific and mention the situation.) I'm sure you are taking an immediate notice.

Please forgive my Father for not treating my body as a Temple (1 Corinthian 6: 19)

I'm asking for you to release me. Keep me in your protection because Satan is a strong temptation in this region.

147

Write your own personal thoughts about what's going through your head

Amen

Quote:

Temperance is a law that has to guide the lives of all Christian. God should be at the center of all our thoughts. His glory will always be kept in mind. It is imperative to stay clear of any influence that could enthrall our minds and distract us away from God. We have holy obligations to God to manage our bodies and control our passions and appetites to ensure to ensure they don't lead to a defilement of purity or holiness or distract us away from the work God has called us to perform. (E. White)

Genius is the supreme quality of perseverance. It is a gift I cannot claim, nor can I claim extra brightness, but the perseverance that everyone can enjoy."

-Woodrow Wilson Woodrow Wilson

Affirmation:

I'll take the chance to consume. The temptation to eat isn't over my capabilities. I will try my best to strengthen my faith by exercising self-control (2 Peter 1:5-7).

I will be thinking of the truth noble honest, pure, gorgeous, admirable, and what is wonderful or worthy of praise. (Philippians 4:8)

--- Woodrow Wilson

I have included two affirmations and quotations on this page because this is the character trait I work towards the all the time! !

Chapter 28: FUNDAMENTALS

How do you define self-talk?

Self-talk refers to the words you speak to yourself typically you don't speak it out loud, it's only the thoughts you talk to yourself about and in some cases, it influences your behavior and feelings.

Self-talk is also defined to be the inner dialogue that you engage in and is affected by the subconscious mind.

The self-talk you engage in reveals your concerns about your beliefs, opinions and thoughts. It can also be positive as well as negative.

The kinds of self-talk that can be negative

Self-talk that is negative falls into the following four categories:

* Personalizing Self-blaming: When you feel that you are responsible for all the things that happen throughout your day. and you accept more responsibility than it is. This is because your mind attempts to blame yourself for all the things that happen within your own life.

* Magnifying: When we all have negative experiences within our lives. For those with hyper-focused self-talk, their mind is always fixated on the negative elements of the situation , and he is unable to see positive aspects.

"* Catastrophizing : This is a nightmare; imagine that your mind is constantly saying things like: "What if you died today? How would you feel if someone else was chattering with you? What if... What happens... What if? ..." Then your mind is constantly imagining things that have nothing to do with have anything to do with the realities of your life.

* Polarizing: From my point of view I believe that polarized thinking can be an imbalance within the individual. Someone who suffers from polarized thinking has a desire for all things to be white, otherwise, everything is black. In this sense, the person suffering from this type of perception believes that if he does not have what he wants the rest of his life is useless and that his life is black. The person who suffers from this distortion decides to have one of two possibilities: A beautiful sweet life, or a awful

151

life. There is no harmony in his thinking and how the world is perceived by him.

How to get rid of self-talk that is negative.

To combat negative self-talk, there's no way to do it overnight If you are looking for a long-term solution. However, you could have a process that works to help you, without having to consult an expert in mental health.

The way you be going through is by identifying the negative thoughts you hold in your head and challenging it using numerous tips and tricks, and finally, establishing positive mental habits such as journaling or meditation.

Chapter 29: IDENTIFY NEGATIVE SELF-TALK

What can you do to identify negative self-talk?

There are a variety of ways to spot negative self-talk. It involves understanding the motivation of your mind telling you. This is either an affirmative or a negative one. There are many ways to accomplish this and you'll learn them today.

Find the commentary that is playing in your head

Take a look at the words you usually have in your head. What do they mean? Are they positive or negative? What affect do they have on your mood and convictions?

It is easy to practice this through sitting at a tranquil space and letting your thoughts run free, and as you go from one moment to the next, keep a record of yourself in the moment of what you thought about in that particular moment.

Accept the fact that your inner voice can be not right.

The issue that you are facing isn't just that you have negative self-talk. The main issue is how you believe about yourself and then accept that as reality. Be sure to not believe the things you believe This is essential for you to experience less self-talk that is negative.

Thoughts are just thoughts, and nothing more than they are thoughts. Be aware of what your mind is constantly telling you. Your mind is in opposition to your own mental health, and so you'll need to deal with it in a manner that doesn't cause you to suffer from issues related in regards to mental wellbeing or feelings.

Utilize your feelings as a signal to look at your thinking

Another way to recognize the negative self-talk you have about yourself is to analyze your emotions to determine how the sensation is created through your thinking.

Consider if the thoughts you're having are creating anxiety What are the phrases and words that you are using (or I would say, your brain uses) which

make you feel anxious in the present If
you do that, you can document it in your
journal.

What can you do to identify the
manifestation of self-talk that can be
negative?

Return to the beginning of the chapter
where we looked at the various types of
negative thoughts, and examine each of
negative self-talk in the four types such
as Magnifying, Personalizing, Polarizing
or Catastrophizing.

Knowing the kind of self-talk that you
have, you will be able to determine the
type of negative self-talk to handle it
using the techniques you're going to
learn in the following chapters.

Chapter 30: CHALLENGE NEGATIVE SELF-TALK

How can you combat self-talk that is negative?

I'll give you easy techniques and steps to end the self-talk you are able to control instantly, without hassle and only with small steps that you can do whenever you feel like you're the "monkey" that is inside of you has been "yelling" towards you.

STEP1

Tell you "STOP" with a loud shout. It may appear silly however, I guarantee you that this is a great way to send your brain an indication to stop. However, remember to not overdo it. You should also avoid talking loudly in a place where all can hear or when you are angry with yourself. Keep it simple.

STEP2

Take a deep breath and breathe deeply. This will allow you to unwind your mind from the turmoil your mind was going through.

STEP3

Keep your breath in for the longest time
you can in the amount you can. It's the
same as what you do during meditation.

STEP4

Make sure you feel like you've
succeeded in doing exactly what you
had been constructing self-defeating
thoughts within your mind.

STEP5

Imagine in your mind the route you will
take to will be able to create your
successful journey

STEP6

Your spiritual goals is to break it down
into steps and then take a deep breath
for each step you take. Make sure you
feel a positive sensation inside you
knowing that you've succeeded in
completing the step. Once you have
done that, affirm the affirmation over
and over and in a loud voice if you are
able.

STEP7

If there isn't any negative self-talk or thoughts in your mind, you may apply these methods throughout the 21 days. In the event of a the gap between, you can take it over again starting from the day you first started to the 21st day.

Chapter 31: MINDFULNESS

Is mindfulness a concept?

Mindfulness is a kind of meditation which requires you to be conscious of your sensations and feeling in the present. This kind of meditation can do every single daylong, and is supposed to be, however it can be challenging, particularly for beginners.

I'm convinced that people from the past, before the invention of technology, were more attentive than us because they had a greater focus. Unfortunately, our age's technology , specifically smartphones and internet technology led us to lose focus and as a result the ability to be mindful became difficult for us.

We are no longer able to appreciate the small things that we used to enjoy like our grandparents did, who were able to enjoy simple things like eating or reading. Today, we can't be aware of how we move We are merely controlled by our autopilot which means that we can't pay attention to our actions. Being focused is a crucial element to be mindful.

Being present in the moment and in the present is a talent and simultaneously an habit. It is a technique to master, and an habit to develop.

Why is mindfulness important for resolving self-talk that is negative?

The self-talk negative you are experiencing is likely because you feel negative feelings regarding something that has happened at some point in your life or perhaps because you're scared of something that could happen in the near future. There is a good chance that we all have bad experiences in the past, and we all often think about negative things that may happen in the future.

If you are spending your day thinking about the past you'll be sad because you allow your emotions to react to something that has already past and will never return to the present.

If you are spending your time contemplating the future, you are likely to be stressed because your feelings be triggered by something which hasn't occurred yet and which doesn't exist in the present.

Don't get in between the two flames or you'll be burnt. Two fires represent both the past and future. If you try to touch one of them you could hurt yourself, so take care.

Our lives are largely governed by our autopilots. Almost everything you do is driven by habit. Of of course, you can utilize habits to your advantage or in a negative manner. Negatively using habits first occurs when you are suffering from bad habits such as addictions. The and the second is when you let them rule your life. The issue when your habits control you is that they are not conscious of them and during the course of an activity, your mind begins traveling back in time into the past and present. This can lead to anxiety, stress, and depression.

Sometimes , when they wish to give you one of these tips, they advise you to not be thinking about the past, but focus on the future and your goals based on what makes you content. That's not my opinion. Also, thinking about the future can cause you to worry and anxieties.

What I say by being present is to be focused on this moment, not today or this week, but just this moment. This is the moment you are studying these lines.

It is what we call mindfulness. It is an excellent skill to acquire for spirituality and maintaining good physical health.

Strategies for Mindfulness

It is important to pay at what's going on around you , and become aware through your senses, for instance the temperature of your surroundings and the smell, sensation of touching, etc.

Be aware of the small things: Let's say you're bored and are in your bed and there's nothing that is interesting to do. This is a great chance to master how to be mindful.

It is possible to do this by paying attention to the small things you've got in your space. For instance, pay close attention to your bed, or your decor. Consider how this came to be. Be aware of the beautiful hues, feel the temperature of the space. Try this at home however, try not to allow your mind to wander back towards the past or to the future.

162

Another option is to perform this while cooking some food in your kitchen. Take a whiff of the food, and focus on the vegetable as you cut it. Everything you do should be contemplative.

Don't be enthralled by the future. It is great to establish goals and create goals, but it's too bad to think all day about the most likely scenario that could happen in the next five years.

The reason that we can't concentrate on the present moment is because we're always interested in what's going to happen next, so my advice to you is to leave this answer be for the future. Future is the sole one that will solve the issue of what's likely to occur.

Be mindful in your everyday activities:

It is important to focus on the things you do during your daily routine, since it will disrupt your autopilot routine. We'll give you some ways you can apply mindfulness to your daily routine:

Food: When you eat take the time to slow down a bit. Also, enjoy eating and concentrating on the flavor and the scent of your food. Make sure to glance at your food and appreciate the design of your food and the color of it as you visualize in your head the steps by which the food took to arrive on your plate.

Walking: If you're walking to somewhere take every step with purpose. Every step you visualize brings an extra boost of energy to your body as well as your mind.

You can also try conscious walking and pay attention to objects around you such as homes, nature, cars and stores, etc. Take in the beautiful views of all the things all around you.

Listening is a fact of life in a world that no one pays attention to our voices. Everyone is focused on what you have to say. Everyone wants to speak and tell what they want to say and impress their experiences. In most instances when someone speaks about us we don't listen, although we do listen to him, but we don't pay attention to him. There is a vast distinction.

When someone speaks to us, we aren't attentive, we aren't focused and we aren't able to look at each other and all of these aspects. The reason I believe this is due to the fact that when someone speaks to us, our minds find it as something that is familiar, so we go back to the autopilot. So that is the issue.

If someone is talking to you, make sure you break your autopilot and stay present whenever someone is talking to you. Here are some ways to do this.

Make eye contact with people who speak to you as this keeps your mind focus on the person. You will be at the forefront of the words he uses. Concentrate on the words he's saying , and try to look at the meaning and build pictures in your mind based on the words he speaks to you. Additionally, try to put yourself like him and try to look through the eyes of your partner and hear to his ears. This is what makes you a great listener.

Working: I'm not aware of what your profession is or what you are doing in your personal life. But I do know that the routine work you perform every day leaves you tired and sad. There is an answer to figure this out.

Be present the moment you get up. Do not waste your time contemplating how your tasks are going to make you tired this day, or what a drag your day will go. Focus on the present moment and I suggest the most effective way to utilize your brain for at the beginning of the day is to reflect about your blessings and being thankful.

Let's suppose that you're working, don't think about what could happen during your job, don't consider your employer, your coworkers or any other thing. Focus on the present moment. While you are working, focus on doing your task, don't let your autopilot take over by forcing you to focus on the past or future.

Is Mindfulness Simple?

As I mentioned, mindfulness is a process that requires skill but simultaneously an habit. Like all skills, it need to practice it often. If you are mindful it is possible to practice "daily mindfulness." If at any point during your day, you notice you thinking about the past or in the future I would like you to take the moment to shift your thoughts into the present. Be careful not to let your mind wander as you think until your feelings react to your thoughts.

The practice of mindfulness should be a regular part of your life and you may be aware that something is wrong with your day when you're not fully present in the moment. You can also create a reminder in any place for you to bring yourself return to the present.

It's not that simple at first But you need to know that it is a skill worth learning since for me, mindfulness is one of the most effective strategies for happiness and to beat your self-talk that is negative.

Chapter 32: Perseverance: I Don't Do Not Give Up

and to self-control, persistence, and perseverance; (I Peter 1:7)

As for your brothers and sisters, they never stop doing what is right.

(Thessalonians 3:13)

I was not being a good person. My blood was boiling in my veins, all I was looking to do was to avenge the full extent of my guilt and let my part in the tale be heard by anyone who would listen.

I confessed to my Lord that I definitely did not consider it fair that I was always the one who needed to humble myself and begin the process of reconciliation with my friend.

Why did I need been the only one who made calls to make the bridge? I had passed the 70-70 threshold.

This was a call to one of teeth for teeth and eye for eye. Do you pray for her safety? (Matthew 5:44) Absolutely not! The line must get drawn someplace. What is the reason God require us to do certain things that we'd rather abandon and let become normal and routine?

We are encouraged to keep going. The definition of perseverance in the dictionary refers to "continued effort to accomplish or accomplish something despite obstacles or failure."

We're never at disadvantage by adhering to God. Whatever is it in your life you must be determined to do, conforming to the Word of God, everything will play for your benefit.

Take a look at how beautiful you look when you keep working out and eating a healthy diet. Similar principles apply to our spiritual health.

It is essential to continue working on it. In the realm of physical fitness, there is no point at which you can sit where you can say, enough is enough. I've completed my workouts for the year. I am now free to go about my business as I like.

I complied and was able to enjoy the peace that comes from forgiveness others. I felt better for it and was more productive over the next months. I decided not to dwell on the suggestions that the Devil often tossed at me about how to get revenge.

Here are 10 amazing Scripture verses that explain the reasons why we should not give up on obeying the call God has given our hearts to perform. We will never be at a disadvantage for following God.

1. In the right season, you'll enjoy the benefits of good luck (Galatians 6:9)

2. You will know the truth, and it will free you (John 8:31, 32)

3. Your power will be restored and you'll fly as an Eagle (Isaiah 40:3)

4. In the end, all you'll be awarded the crown of eternal the eternal life (James 1:2)

5. You'll be extremely productive (John 15:4,5)

6. You will be able to ask for what want and it will be done to the person who asks (John 15:7)

7. It can make you a more pleasant person because it will strengthen your character. This is the only thing you'll be able to take with you to Heaven (Romans 5:3-4)

8. God's promises will be fulfilled (Hebrew 10:36)

9. Your efforts will be rewarded (2 Chronicles 15:7)

10. You'll have eternal life (Romans 2:7)

The best part is that you'll be complete,
mature and never lacking anything
(James 1:4)

Prayer:

Father, I am grateful to you for being
extremely accommodating to me. Who
can be an God like you who is patient
and full of mercy? (Numbers 14:18)
You've fought long with me.

I've fallen numerous times during my
Christian journey however, in my
weaknesses the strength of your faith
has perfection.

The most successful men and women in
the Lord are always those that haven't
abandoned their dreams. Keep me in
your hands and never quit in all you
have made me to be.

In particular , I ask (mention the areas
of your life that you're struggling to
overcome) that you grant me the
courage to fly like an eagle.

I want to thank you for the numerous
occasions that I've persevered. I am

sure that all good things originate from you, and it was you who helped me keep going.

I am thankful that even in this moment of difficulty, I am able to trust in you Lord and you will rekindle my faith. I will fly like an eagle. will run and not become tired and I will walk and not give up. (Isaiah 40:31)

Write your own personal thoughts about what's in your head

Amen

Quote:

"Never ever give up" -- Winston Churchill

Affirmation:

I could be thrown seven times down but I will get up to the top (Proverbs 24:16)

Chapter 33: Godliness: Every One Does It

It is also known that in the final days, dangerous times will come. Because men will be self-centered, lustful proud, covetous prideful, blasphemers, unfaithful to parents, unthankful and unholy. ...... With a form of godliness, yet denying the power of it and thereby turning away. (2nd Timothy 3:1-5)

Peter became angry and appeared to exhale flames and smoke like an injured dinosaur whose territory was taken over. In the course of the discussion, he grumbled under his breath, clearly expressing his anger. His territory was being invaded, but Charles was of a different opinion of his. Much to Peters displeasure, Charles expressed his opinions quite arrogantly, proving to all that he had a better idea. After the meeting was over and both men left with a huge puff. What was a United Nations meeting attempting to help warring parties find an agreement that is peaceful? This was not an event at a church I was there with 12 other saints of God.

The fact that everyone around us isn't acting like the Christian they're supposed to be, it shouldn't lead us to believing that our behavior is acceptable and acceptable with God.

If we take a look at Jesus and contemplate his life, we'll naturally learn how to behave towards other people. I believe that this is the essence of what Christianity is about. It's never been about the way others treat you, however how you treat them.

In the Garden of Gethsemane shortly prior to the time that Christ was crucified, leaders of the religious order and Roman soldiers gathered to as a prized prey using their swords and guns. This was a man who's sole crime was that he loved people. He cared for, healed the sick, banished demons and made the lives of people meaningful. However, he was now being deceived from one of his close circle, Judas. Another of his close friends, Peter was about to be furiously denial him, and his friends were also about to leave him.

John chapter 18 provides an insight into Christ's divine traits. He heals the servants of the High Priests with his ear, which Peter had cut off to defend Jesus and is quiet and humble. He does

not let insults out of his mouth. He could
have summoned angels in a horde to
defend him and made minced flesh of
his opponents, but due to his deep love
for the human race He chose to endure
the pain on the cross.

He realized that He could bring mankind
return to God and that made it even
more important.

Being a Christian nowadays means
more than simply studying the bible and
performing certain religious rituals. It's
about possessing the same powers that
has made Jesus an amazing person,
and the capacity to be a very nice
person. Christ displayed his gifts from
the Spirit throughout his life all the way
to death. There was no end to his joy,
love peace, patience, compassion,
kindness, goodwill in his faithfulness,
gentleness, and self-control. (Galatians
5:22-22) It was the kind of friend,
brother or coworker you'd want to be
able to

God via the crucified Christ has given
us the power to transform into Christ as
we are and to be godly. It's not too
difficult. Your character should improve
in these ways. It is not possible to be

Christians who display more of the fleshly fruits than the fruit that are of the heart. The fleshly fruits are sexual immorality, impurity , extreme sensuality, idolatry, witchcraft and hostility. They also have bitter conflicts and jealousy. They also show outbursts of anger and lack of unity discord, cliquishness, envying, drinking as well. (Galatians 5:16-17)

The Bible warns us that during the coming days there will be those who claim to be part of God but deny the God-given power that makes them godly. We reject this power because we believe we are unable to display the fruit of the spirit , or provide reasons for why we can't be patient, kind and gentle with one another. Our goal is being Christ like. This isn't impossible since when God requires us to take action, he gives us the power to help us to fulfill that call. Through the daily in baptism by the Holy Spirit, we are transformed into the image of Christ.

Prayer:

My Father in Heaven, thank you for all things that can be accomplished. You are God of the Lord, All powerful. You strengthen me and help me walk with perfect. You transform me into an animal's feet and I am able to reach the top of the hill. I am grateful that you prepare me to fight; my arms are able to bend into bows made of bronze. I am given an oath of triumph as well as your left hand is there to support me. You bend down to make me more powerful and you widen the way under me so that my ankles aren't rotate.

Thank you for being a part of my life to sanctify me every day to be better than you. I am grateful to you and praise you for the amazing work you're accomplishing in my own life.

Please forgive me for (state specific character flaws you've recently displayed) my non-Christlike manners. I am grateful that when I confess my sins, you're faithful and kind to forgive me for all my transgressions (Psalm 3:3) (I John 1:19)

Lord, sometimes I struggle to live like you and to forgive those who deliberately planning against me, and it is hurtful. It is difficult for me to be kind to my friends who have disappointed me, while being patient with my kids and loving when I am screamed at.

Let me be as you in all negative situations that I face in the course of life.

I am thankful to you because you've answered my questions and have transformed me into a beautiful vessel that is pleasing to your eyes.

I have more fun living my life through becoming as like you.

Include your own thoughts of what's going through your head

Amen

Quote:

The secret to godliness is not knowledge, but faith (Woodrow Kroll)

Affirmation:

Today, I will through the strength by the Holy Spirit, become peace-loving, joyful, loving and patient. I will be kind, compassionate and loving, gentle, and self-controlled. There is no limit on how much I can show these traits.

Conclusion

I want to thank you for reading this book. I hope that you gained something from this brief book. Everything you want in your life begins with you Your relationship with yourself can lead to many positive things within your life. I encourage you to begin now on to give yourself reverence and respect. Be aware that you will never be free of yourself as it is the only place that you can be. planets. True beauty is within you and self-worth is the way you treat yourself. Do not let other people's opinions influence your perception of what you are worth Always hold your self-esteem high. It doesn't matter what are going through at the moment. When you wake up each day make sure you remind yourself that you're wonderfully created It's a good idea to say that you will never cause harm, always remember that you're not on your own Your self-image is stronger than you could ever imagine Say beautiful thoughts to yourself. Don't wait for others to be kind to you before you begin appreciating yourself. Being 100% committed to yourself is the obligation you owe to yourself. Find your self-image so that things will go according to plan your way in the near future. You've probably told yourself numerous negative things about yourself. Everyone has been guilty of it and as you're done reading these books "I need you to affirm that to you. Today I promise to continue to love myself regardless of how others view me. I will be a loving person to myself to the end of the road. This can be pinned anywhere in your home , where you will see it each day. Repeat the phrase as many times as you want. If you don't have friends who inspire you, I suggest you to make new acquaintances. Self-love is the first step, take the time to be yourself, there is no one who is more than you do. Get started today and begin to truly love yourself.

Thanks and Best of Luck Thanks and Good Luck !

www.ingramcontent.com/pod-product-compliance
Lightning Source LLC
Chambersburg PA
CBHW060334030426
42336CB00011B/1330